Good shift!

JENNIFER POWERS

Powerhouse Publishing

Good shift!
Copyright © 2020 Powerhouse, Inc.
www.jenniferpowers.com

Cover design by Ranilo Cabo
Back cover photo by Kathryn Elsesser

Published by:
Powerhouse Publishing, a division of Powerhouse, Inc.
Portland, OR

Printed in USA

ISBN: 978-0-9854738-9-1

For the
ever-changing,
adaptable
you

TABLE OF CONTENTS

PREFACE

Since writing the best-selling book *Oh, shift!,* I've spent nearly a decade delivering keynotes at conferences and corporate events. I've spoken to hundreds of thousands of professionals all over the world, reminding them that they can live a more joyful life and sharing tools to help them do it.

Before I speak, I always chat with the event planners to get a picture of what each audience needs. During these visits, I've determined that despite the many differences in the audiences themselves, there's one thing that almost all audience members struggle with – DEALING WITH CHANGE.

That's no surprise, as research shows that 77% of HR practitioners and leaders report that their organization is in a constant state of change.

Change is hard and people don't like it. Many dislike it so much that they'll outright resist it. In fact, whole companies have been brought down when employees within a company actively sabotage efforts to reform or grow.

This resistance leads to all sorts of problems for the org like decreased performance, high turnover, loss of revenue, lawsuits, and so on. Not to mention how it can affect the individual. Constantly having to deal with change in the workplace is stressful. Many take that stress home with them and it affects every aspect of their lives, including their health and their relationships.

The damage can be extensive.

And yes, plenty of change management programs are executed with positive intent. But research now shows that 85% of organizations have experienced an unsuccessful change management initiative in the past two years. I wonder if it's because most of them use fancy models with blue circles and squares and are mostly created by people in academia that speak to the needs of the organization rather than to the needs of the individuals within the organization.

These acronym-laden models are often a top-down approach focusing on communication, strategy, structure, vision, or core values; and involve complicated, lengthy processes that look at the whole organization, but too often fail to focus on the individual parts of the whole - the people.

As a coach, I have seen time and time again that if you prioritize and take care of the *individual* working parts of any organization (the people) then the *whole* organization naturally functions at a higher level.

When an organization goes through change, performance suffers. So doesn't it make sense to support the performers? Of course it does. And that's why I wrote this book.

I wrote this book because I believe organizations will benefit from prioritizing the personal development of their individual contributors by giving them tools to be their best selves...especially in environments of constant change.

Making personal development a priority creates nothing short of a WIN-WIN-WIN.

The *organization* wins because when each of its parts are improved, the sum of its parts improves-which usually translates to a healthier bottom line. *You* win because you're more equipped, less stressed, and just plain healthier. And *your family and social life* win because you are no longer emotionally drained from all the shift that's going on at work.

So yes, it may be difficult to navigate change, but by offering tools to the ones that matter most, it's possible to successfully go through change and come out a winner.

In this book you'll find tools. Lots of them. Tools that help you get back in the driver's seat and stand in your power. But this book can't do it alone. It needs YOU. It requires YOU to have an open mind and a willingness to stretch a bit. Not a lot, but a bit.

Some of the stuff you may dig, some parts may turn you off. No big. Take what serves you and leave behind what doesn't.

If you've read *Oh, shift!* you know that you can choose to have more joy in your life by thoughtfully choosing your words and your reactions. Well, this book is no different.
Your choices. Your reality. Your life. This is *your* work.

I promise that if you carefully examine and apply the principles in this book you will be far more prepared to deal with any change that comes your way. So commit to sitting with the concepts. Challenge them. Talk about them.

If you're really serious, give some extra time to the Reflection Questions you'll find along the way. You can answer them yourself or bring them to a meeting and answer them as a group. Either way, do the work because you want to.
Nobody's making you do anything.

This is your choice.

Everything is your choice. Keep reading or don't. Put these ideas into practice or don't. If you never apply anything in this book you will totally be ok. But if you're someone who wants to be more than ok, more in control, and more relaxed amidst change, then give yourself an hour and see what's possible.
You've already started reading, and if you follow this through to the end you may just end up winning. And you deserve to win.
You really do.

Jennifer Powers

SHIFT
IS
REAL

Shift \ ˈshift \

: to ex-**change** for or replace by another

: to **change** the place, position, or direction of

: to make a **change**

: to go through a **change**

L isa was eighteen when she got her tattoo. A snake wrapped around her left ankle, slithering up her calf. She loved it. What's not to love?

It was sexy, rebellious and just what she needed to piss off her parents.

Nearly a decade later, on her wedding day, she found herself cursing the decision she had made in her youth as she blotted make up over the snake that was peeking out of her bright white gown. Sigh.

Not long after turning thirty-nine, Lisa woke up one day, looked at her husband of eleven years and realized the commitment they promised to uphold was barely holding itself together. He just wasn't the same guy she married.

And she wasn't the same girl.

Forty-eight brought her an empty nest. It felt like a swift kick in the stomach as she sent her only daughter off to college. After all, that was her baby girl.

So. Much. Change.

With over a half a century under her belt, change was no stranger to Lisa. In fact, by this point she thought she was pretty good at dealing with change.

Until she went through the *biggest* CHANGE. OF. LIFE. She was fifty-four.

Hello menopause.

One thing you can always count on is change.

Moods change
Styles change
Weather changes
Politics change
Minds change
Technology changes
Partnerships change
Travel plans change
Opinions change
Children change
Climate changes
Bodies change
You change

And thank goodness. I mean, imagine if suddenly things just stopped changing.
We would hate that.
Why?

Change evolves us.

And we humans love to evolve. It's actually what we're here to do. Procreate, evolve, procreate, evolve. If things stopped changing, if WE stopped changing, WE would stop evolving. Then we'd just be procreating all day, which sounds fun, but we'd also still be dragging our knuckles, hunting antelope, gathering berries and carrying little hairy babies on our backs.

Eek.

I think Chuck Darwin said it best...

"It is not the strongest of the
species that survives,

nor the most
intelligent,

but the one
most responsive
to change."

Change is inevitable.

You can't hide from it.
You can't stop it.
You can't avoid it.
But you can (and you will) (and you do) try to resist it.

We hate change.

We all do.
No exceptions.

If you think you like change then put this book down, close your
eyes and imagine any of the following:

> Your regular commute to work now involves two new
> toll roads *and* a detour
> Your local grocery store closed
> Your new grocery store doesn't carry your brand of
> anything
> Your doctor retired
> Your twenty-five year-old son just moved back in
> Your favorite off-leash dog park just became on-leash
> Starbucks went out of business
>
> Yeah, you can almost hear change saying,

"How do ya like me NOW?"

Change sucks.

So we resist it.
We want to fight it, beat it into submission and
tell it to go home.
We don't want to see it, know it, feel it.
And for good reason.

Humans are creatures of habit.
We don't like to step outside of our comfort zone because we're
also creatures of *comfort*. We love routine, the expected, the path
of least resistance. We feel our most confident in the easy, breezy
state of familiarity and predictability.

Familiar is safe.
You know how to survive in the current conditions.
But change 'em and things can start to feel
uncertain, unstable, scary.

Familiar is also easy.
Our brains work best on autopilot. We expend very little energy
when we do things the way we've always done them.
But change 'em and now we have to think. Concentrate.
Learn how to be successful in the new environment.
This makes us expend calories. Brain calories. And we are hard-
wired to conserve calories (you know, for survival).
Seriously, no joke. THIS is why change is so damn hard for us.
It makes us use energy that we are programmed to
conserve and reserve...
for our survival.

You resist change
to keep yourself safe,
comfy, and
most importantly
to avoid anything
that requires
an extra expenditure
of energy that
could be used for hunting antelope
and fighting off opposing tribes.

You are so human.

And what humans might not get is that...

Change is good.

Check it.
Change prevents stagnation,
boredom, numbing, and complacency.

Change washes away the old,
worn, and weary.

Ushers in the fresh and new.

Change solves problems.
Moves us forward.

Blooms the flower, turns the leaves, and
sets the sun.

Change keeps us alive.
Renews our cells.
Keeps us hopeful.

Change carries us through life.
And makes it better.

Not convinced?

Think of how the world
would be if these things
NEVER changed:

>   Civil rights
>   The Model T
>   Dental treatments
>   Two-year olds
>   The Commodore 64
>   Nazi Germany
>   The stock market
>   Your underwear
>   The mullet

But the best part about change?

It forces you to...

learn more so you're not stupid
experience more so your life is richer
get better at things you suck at
exercise your brain and avoid dementia
challenge yourself to be more flexible
discover hidden talents you never
knew you had
shift from resistance to flow

To test this for yourself, turn the page.

Challenge yourself to complete the following exercise
to experience doing something differently,
the fun you can have with it,
and how it feels to find flow when you're in it.

Note: This is just an exercise. It's meant to challenge you and
it's your choice whether you take on the challenge or not.

Read this page from the <u>bottom up</u> and <u>right to left</u>...

.thgir m'I kniht I... ?thgir I ma rO ?thgir I mA .doog os
os leef lliw ksat drawkwa siht gnitelpmoc dna dne eht
gnirean era uoy esnes uoy woN !egnahc fo trofmocsid
eht hguorht dehsup dna raf siht ti edam ev'uoY .won uoy
gnippots on s'erehT ?nuf elttil a neve ebyaM ?thgir ,rei-
sae gnitteg s'tI !og uoy ta kool tub elbatrofmocnu si ti
,seY .prahs ti peek lliw hcihw niarb ruoy fo trap wen a
tuokrow nac uoy ,tib elttil a tsuj rof enoz trofmocsid eht
ni yats ot flesruoy egnellahc uoy fi tuB

.od ot sgniht retteb htiw nosrep ysub a era uoy dna elbatrofmocnu dna tnereffid si ti sulP .enod si gnidaer
yaw eht ton s'ti esuaceb esicrexe yllis a hcus gniod tsiser
yam uoY .siht thgif yam uoY

Now, you either **started and quit** that exercise, **started and finished** or just **skipped the whole thing**.
Which one was it?
What does that say about you and how you deal with change?

If you started and quit before finishing the exercise, you are a bit averse to doing things differently and will benefit from this book because it will challenge you to step out of your comfort zone where you prefer to stay 62% of the time.*

If you started and finished the exercise you are pretty good with change and enjoy the inherent challenge that it offers. Two thirds of this book* will strongly resonate with you and you will feel affirmed quite often.

If you skipped the exercise entirely, kudos for exercising your power to choose! You too will feel affirmed quite often throughout the book AND will benefit from stretching outside your comfort zone which you choose to stay in 8 out of 10 times.*

Now, the point of this exercise is to simply:
- CHANGE the way you do something (read)
- feel the discomfort
- discover how you manage/react/respond

Pretty cool, huh?

*These statistics are absolutely unscientific and totally made up.

It's funny.

Even when some inherently good shift happens, with it can come some consequential bad shift.

- Like reading that page backwards. Sure, it made you feel cool (and like a ninja) but that's time you will literally never get back.

    - Anyone would agree that getting a promotion is good shift. But having to manage those who were once your equals may not be so easy.

- What better shift is there than bringing your first child into the world? But say goodbye to bar hopping and all-night rodeos.

    - And yes, they finally fired that bad-apple-bully in your department, but somebody's gotta pick up the slack that hag left behind.

Ah, life. It never fails to find the balance.
But that's ok, because you get it. It's all the same.
It's just shift.

    And it happens.

Even funnier.

Why did the toll booth operator lose his job?

He couldn't deal with change.

Stop expecting change to suck.
It doesn't *always* suck.

Stop wishing it away.
It's *not* going away.

Stop believing you're going to hate change.
You may absolutely *love* it.

Stop thinking things aren't going to change.
You won't be so *pissed* when they do.

Stop hoping YOU won't change.
You are changing as you read this sentence.

Change sucks or it doesn't.
You should love it or hate it.
It can help you or hurt you.

The goal is not to convince you of any of the above.

Instead, this book is meant to help you navigate the
inevitable changes that are **undoubtedly** going to
take place in your **foreseeable** future.

Shift is happening my friend, and you'll want to be prepared to
deal with it before it deals with YOU.

Let's do this.

REFLECTION QUESTIONS

How do you feel when things in your world change?

What change are you dealing with right now?*

How are you reacting to this change?

How is this change helping you grow?

These questions can help you apply
the principles found in this book to your life and work.
Feel free to answer them on your own or with colleagues.
Write your answers or speak them aloud.
Could you just skip them?
Sure, but that would be like sitting for a seven-course meal and
only eating four. You'll leave the table hungry and cheated.
Plus, you deserve it all. Soup to nuts.
So dig in. I dare you.

*If you think you're NOT dealing with change right now, think again.
Everything is changing all the time.

THE THING YOU FORGET

Omar was good at his job. Working for the same company for fifteen years, he was comfortable in his role and very confident in his ability to get things done efficiently. His creative ideas were welcomed, and he was given a ton of freedom to lead his team in the way he saw fit.
Life was good.

Then it happened.

His employer went through a merger, creating a change in ownership AND leadership, and Omar hated it.

Suddenly he was told he would have to "do things differently".
His autonomy was lost and stress was the soup du jour, every jour.
What was once a laid-back, easy-breezy job, became a big, hot, ugly mess that Omar began to resent.

Within the first month of the take-over, Omar called me for some coaching to help him deal with this massive change that was throwing him into, as he called it, "a tailspin".

In our very first session I heard it. It went something like this...

*"I just can't believe this! Everything has been taken from me.
It feels like they made me row myself out to the middle of the lake and then took my paddles away. What am I supposed to do now? I'm stuck in this mess and there's nothing I can do about it."*

As his coach, my job was easy.

*"Left with no paddles. Stuck. Nothing you can do.
What might you be forgetting, Omar?"*

It's easy to forget.

I know.
When shift happens, you may be a bit like Omar.
So busy feeling hurt, frustrated, frazzled or angry
that you forget about your birth-given superpower.

The one and only thing that
NO ONE CAN EVER TAKE FROM YOU.

The get-out-of-jail-free card that you can always
play. Any day. Any time. Even if it's not your turn.

The gift of all gifts that you can give to yourself,
when you remember that you have it to give....

The power to choose.

Ahh, choices.

You make hundreds every day,
dozens every hour.

When to wake up
When to leave
What to wear
What to eat
How to act
Who to call
What to buy
Where to go
How long to stay
Whether to exercise
What time to go to bed

Based on the choices you make,
your day will play out one way or another.

Based on how your day goes,
your collective week will be determined.

Based on the kind of week you have,
your month will follow suit.

That flows into years and, of course, life.

Your choices make up your life.
And the best part?

When

shift happens,

you have

a choice.

The moment shift happens,
you get to choose how you will think about it,
talk about it and react to it.

AND...

The more thought you put into
making those choices, the more equipped you are to
deal with the shift.

AND...

The more equipped you are to
deal with the shift, the less it can ruffle
your pretty little feathers.

Ka-kaaaaaw.

W hen you forget you have choices, you can't see them.

And when you can't see your choices, you can't make them.

This happens to Caroline on a daily. Ever since her boss started making her come to work an hour earlier she hasn't been able to get in her morning workout. She feels so frustrated because she's gaining weight, and has no problem blaming the extra padding on her boss.

Ah, sweet Caroline. Lest you forget, your boss may control your schedule, but she can never control when and if you work out.

That my dear, is your choice.

Good times never seemed so good.

Thanks to your incredible
superpower to choose,
shift can be
easy,
difficult,
awesome,
annoying, or
a jolly good time.

It's all up to you.

It's totally your choice.
Because it's totally your life.

REFLECTION QUESTIONS

What situation are you dealing with now that feels like you have no choice?

Is it true that you have no choice?

What choices do you <u>really</u> have?

What fear keeps you from making those choices?

That last one's a doozy
so you may need to talk it out with someone.
But it's so worth it because you'd be amazed to know
how often fear rules the roost.

We're all a bit cock-a-doodle-doo-doo.
But get to the bottom of that fear
and you'll be king cock.

THE CHOICES YOU HAVE

Choice #1
WHO
YOU ARE

Have you ever said statements like these...?

"I'm miserable at work because my **boss** is a jerk."

"I would do yoga if I had more **time**."

"I'd work harder if **they** paid me more."

"I'd get more sales if I had more **leads**."

"If the **economy** were better, I'd be able to find a job."

"Damn **politicians**!"

Of course you have.
You're human, with a pulse.
But here's a memo you don't want to miss...

Whenever you make statements like these
you are pointing your bony little finger at
other PEOPLE and THINGS and holding
THEM responsible for
YOUR reality being the way it is.

You are BLAMING
everyone and everything else
for YOUR
outcomes,
feelings,
actions,
reactions,
and choices.

And when you do that

you are choosing to play the Victim.

I'm pretty familiar with playing the Victim.

Like when I'm driving and the person in front of me is moving like a snail through molasses, it's just too easy to blame him for making me feel (<u>fill in blank with any nasty emotion</u>).

> *"If he would just drive like a 'normal person'*
> *I wouldn't be so pissed."*

I may also hold him responsible for, um, anything.

> *"UGH! This guy's gonna make me*
> *late for my meeting!"*

And I rarely miss an opportunity to blow my horn and blow off some steam.

> *"GET OUT OF MY WAAAAAYYY!"*

Or my good old Victim-y standby...

> *"WHY ARE YOU DOING THIS TO ME?!"*

If any of this sounds slightly familiar, read on.
If it doesn't, you probably have fewer pent up emotions.
Kudos.
But you should still keep reading.

When you choose to be a Victim, you're literally
GIVING YOUR POWER AWAY
to the person or thing you hold responsible for
your state of affairs.

They don't even ask for it.
You just give it to them.

And there are so many good reasons to hold on to your power.

First, your power is way too valuable to give away.
Think diamond-encrusted-Taj Mahal valuable.

And the more power you give away,
the less you'll have to reach your goals.
Imagine running three marathons, back-to-back in the desert.
You gonna give someone your *water*?

Oh, and with less power, your performance will suffer too.
The 3-cyl. Geo Metro comes to mind. Ugh.

But you know this, right?

So, here's something...

You are not a Victim.

I repeat. You are not a Victim...
unless you choose to be.

You get to choose
who you will be in any moment of every day.
You can choose to
be the Victim and give your power away.
Or you could hold onto your power and choose to
be the Victor.

To be a Victor you have to take *some* responsibility for the way
your day, week, month, year, life is turning out.
After all, you must be somewhat responsible.
It's YOUR life.

See, once you realize that you own a chunk of the responsibility in
any situation, you can take more control of that situation, arrive
to your meeting on time and avoid acting like a fart face.

But this is gonna take a little effort because most of us have been
at this Victim thing for some time. So be gentle with yourself as
you break in the new Victor boots.

Meanwhile, here are some ways you can check in to see if you're
choosing to play the victim or the shift-kicking victor.

FEELINGS

Victims hold other people and things responsible for the
way they feel. They relish any opportunity to blame their
misery, sadness, anger, etc. on others.
This keeps them small and powerless.

Steve, a long-time bank employee, chooses to be a victim
whenever he blames his boss for his frustrations at work.
He says if his boss trusted him more
he'd feel more motivated.
Steve is giving away his precious personal power to his boss.

Victors recognize that they get to choose
how they want to feel.
For Steve to be a Victor, he would have to take responsibility
and ownership for the way he feels.
Sure, his boss may be a control freak,
and Steve can't control that.
But he can control how he chooses to feel
about his boss *and* his job.

Steve could begin to take his power back by asking himself,
"How do I choose to feel?"

The truth is,
no *thing,*
event, or *person*
has the power
to make you feel
frustrated, underpaid, overworked,
unorganized, unappreciated,
unsuccessful,
fat, ugly,
sick or
tired.

Only you.
It's your choice.

And another thing...

Stop relying on everyone else to make you feel happy, worthy, valued, appreciated, and awesome.

There's no way you're going to excel ANYWHERE if you sit around waiting for everyone else to make you feel good.

IT'S NOT THEIR JOB.

And even if it *was* their job, some people are so shitty at it you could go grey waiting for them to figure out how to give you the words of affirmation and appreciation you need.

DON'T. WAIT. FOR. THEM.

You deserve better than that. The only person you can count on for affirmation and appreciation is you.

Be your own boss, applesauce.

Pat your own damn self on the back.

You totally deserve it.

ACTIONS

Victims make no connection between their
actions and their reality.

Karen, a department manager, chooses to be the Victim when
she complains that her employees never come to her
when there's a problem.
She says that she's always "in the dark".
This lack of communication obviously keeps Karen
from being an effective leader.

Victors understand that their
actions create and affect their reality.
And they are brave enough to investigate how.

To be a Victor, Karen could try to identify the connection
between her actions and her employees'
reluctance to come to her when there's trouble.

Karen could ask herself,
*"What part do I play in my staff feeling
reluctant coming to me?"*

OPTIONS

Victims believe and act as if they have no options.

Remember Omar?
He played the Victim when he said he was "stuck in a job"
that made him so miserable.
Omar clearly forgot about his superpower to choose.
It didn't occur to him to identify his options
because he didn't think he had any.

Victors recognize and exercise their options.
Victors never feel stuck.
They know that they always have another option.
Often several.

So for Omar to step out of the Victim role, he could ask
himself, *"What options do I have in this situation?"*
When he recognizes that he has options, he can take
his power back and have more control
over his emotional well-being and job satisfaction.

Shazaaam.

Until someone literally has a gun to your head,

you can't sit there and say you have no options.*

I call bull-shift!

You ALWAYS have options and

you ALWAYS have choices.

The question is
are you exercising them?

*If someone really does have a gun to your head, my apologies.
That sounds awful.

When you have to deal with a big or small shift, it's easy to hold that shift responsible for your feelings, actions, reactions, and choices.

You may want to blame the change in policy for your poor performance, or the change in deadline for your failure to meet it.

New leadership might be the perfect target (read: scape-goat) to blame your unhappiness on.

It is definitely easier to blame abc on xyz rather than admitting you had a role in it.

But know this…
By holding everyone and everything else responsible for your life being the way it is, you are holding yourself back from reaching your full potential.
You're staying small. And you're not small.
Stop acting like you are.

Take your power back and watch what happens.
Watch yourself bloom, grow, and thrive.
Watch yourself be your BEST self.
You can be a Victor and a very powerful one,
if you choose.

REFLECTION QUESTIONS

Who or what do you tend to blame for your feelings, actions or choices?

What change are you blaming right now?

What can you do to own some responsibility and take your power back?

These are not easy questions to answer.
So go sit down with a cup of tea, a bag of chips,
or a fifth of whiskey and dive in.
The deeper you go, the more power you get back
because self-awareness is your friend.

A PSA: Not looking at who you are and how you show up in the world will always keep you from being your best self.

If you wanna tune up the engine, ya gotta look under the hood.

Vrooom.

Choice #2
WHAT
YOU SAY

Joe wants to build a house so he sets out to order his building materials (lumber and whatnot).

Depending on the quality of the materials he chooses, Joe can build a good house that is solid, reliable, and comfortable or a house that's shabby, drafty, and uncomfortable.

Joe has lots of choices
and the choices he makes
will definitely affect his results.

Choosing materials to build a house is kinda like choosing your words to create your reality.

Your words make up the foundation
and the framework of the house
you call your life.

Choose shitty materials, build a shitty house.
Choose shitty words, build a shitty life.

There's no getting around it.

The quality of Joe's house
depends on the materials he chooses.
And the quality of your life
depends on the words you choose.

Choosing quality words over cheap substitutes is easy though. We actually do this all the time.

When talking to children, old people and CEOs, we may tend to choose the more "appropriate" alternatives over our lazy *slanguage*.

"Yeah" becomes *"Yes."*

"You bet" becomes *"Certainly."*

"Dunno" becomes *"I'm not quite sure."*

Or we censor our colorful language and opt for the G-rated version. (Think: *heck, darn, rear-end or shut the front door.*)

'Nuff said.

Why do we do that?

Because the words we choose can make us
better.

Better role models for our children.
Better candidates in an interview.
Better team members at work.
Better guests at dinner parties.
Better prospects on first dates.

You can choose your words
to make your whole life
better.

You are if you say you are.
It will if you say it will.

Say you'll never get the promotion. Done.
Say you're gonna close the sale and you will.
Say you're gonna blow the interview. OK. No problem.
Say it'll suck and it will.
Say it's awesome and it is.
Say it's never gonna work and it won't.

You call it.
It's your choice.
It's your life.

J ane is a busy account executive whose numbers are decent but not as high as they need to be. She struggles with certain parts of the sales process and finds herself frustrated month after month when she doesn't meet her quota. Not surprisingly, when someone asks Jane how she's doing, her go-to response is often either:

"Not so great."
or
"Work sucks!"

What Jane doesn't know is that, as harmless as these responses may seem, her words are creating the reality that she loves to complain about *and* the results she's getting (or not getting)

And here's why...

||||||||||||||||||||||||||||||||||||||||||||||||||||||||||| 63 |||||||||||

What Jane says will influence what she thinks.

What Jane thinks will influence how she feels.

How Jane feels will influence what she does.

What Jane does will influence her results.

Every time.

Here's how things are playing out for Jane…

She chooses to **say**…
"Work sucks!"

Which makes her **think**…
My life literally sucks for 40+ hours a week.

Which makes her **feel**…
Sucky.

Which makes her **do**…
A sucky job.

Which **results** in…
Sucky numbers.

You get it.

And this is true for everyone, everywhere, every day.
What you say matters
and it will always make the bed that you lay in.

Imagine that the company you work for made a change to the such and such policy and you totally disagree with their decision to do so.

You choose to **say**...
"What idiots!"

Which makes you **think**...
I work for a bunch of idiots.

Which makes you **feel**...
Superior, egoic, victimized, frustrated.

Which makes you **do**...
Recklessly spew out your opinion about the "stupid policy change" to anyone who will listen.

Which **results** in...
You being one of those miserable, opinionated, Negative-Nellies that others don't want to be around.
(And you wonder why they aren't asking you to step into a leadership role. Hmmm.)

Now imagine the same scenario: They made the change and you still don't agree with it, but this time:

You choose to **say**...
"Hmmm. That's interesting."

Which makes you **think**...
I wonder what they had in mind when they made that change.

Which makes you **feel**...
Curious, interested, mature.

Which makes you **do**...
Spend your time trying to understand the reasons for such a change.

Which **results** in...
You being seen as a thoughtful, curious, intelligent person that others want to hang around...and promote.

Now that's some good shift.

Choosing your **words** means choosing your **reality**.

When shift happens
    and you intentionally choose what you'll say about it,
        you can become the captain of your ship.
Sailing the high seas, ready for anything that comes your way.
    Rough waters don't scare you.
        Your words are your sail and they can guide you to
        smoother, beautiful, clear blue waters.

                                    Ahoy matey.

REFLECTION QUESTIONS

What do you tend to say when shift happens?

What word or phrase do you want to stop saying because it isn't giving you the results you want?

What word or phrase could you say in its place?

So, you're either answering these thoughtful questions or just skipping them. I get it. I do the latter sometimes too. But reading the questions isn't going to get you where you want to go. You have to answer them. So if you skipped them, go back. Take a minute. You deserve it. And if it helps, here's a shortcut. Just fill in the blanks.

"When shift happens, instead of saying _____

I will say _____.

Bam.

Choice #3
HOW
YOU REACT

T he other day I was walking my dog and, as luck had it, I stepped in a pile of poo. Right there, in the middle of the sidewalk, now smeared all over the sole of my brand-new sneakers.

I was furious. I mean, come on people! Do the right thing! Embarrassed and angry, I spewed a few obscenities under my breath, then noticed a woman walking toward me.
I took advantage to let off some steam.

"Can you believe this? %!#*ing idiots! Some people are so inconsiderate. What's wrong with the world today? Some jackass thought it would be okay to just leave their dog's sh*t behind hoping someone else would pick it up. Well guess what? (I cupped my mouth to make a megaphone out of my hands and shouted to the sky) 'Your mother doesn't live here!!!!!!'"

The lady looked at me, panic stricken, and said...

"I'm so sorry. I ran out of baggies and had to run across the street to grab one. That was, um...that was my bad."

No lady. That was <u>my</u> bad. You may have left it there. But I stepped in it...big time.

Shift doesn't happen TO you.

Shift just happens.

Your job is not to control the shift,
stop the shift, or even fight the shift.

Your job is to choose

how you react
to the shift.

Because the way you react to shift
determines whether or not
it's gonna hit the fan.

Imagine.

A medium-sized paper company goes through a re-org.

Stanley, Kelly and Meredith all get laid off.

Stanley takes his severance and retires to Florida.

Kelly sees this as an opportunity and applies
for the new Assistant to the Regional Manager role.

Meredith freaks out and drowns herself in vodka.

Eleven months later...
Kelly wins Assistant to the Regional Manager of the Year,
Stanley is living large in St. Petersburg,
and Meredith is headed to rehab.

The shift was the same for all three people - the company
went through a re-org and they lost their jobs.
There was nothing any of them could do to control or
prevent that from happening.

But each of them had control over how they reacted
to it. They each reacted differently and they each got different
results.

Easy.

That's what she said.

REACTIONS = REALITY

Your reactions create your reality.

Choose a negative reaction and
you will create a negative reality.

Choose a positive reaction and
you will create a positive reality.

"But Jen, how am I supposed to choose a positive reaction when some really bad shift goes down?"

I'm so glad you asked.

But first, a trip to the head.

You are head driven.
You mostly live in your head and you go there for approval,
rationale, decisions, and of course, your reactions.

In your head you decide how you'll
react to any shift that happens.

But here's the rub.

Two people live in your head and they are both **YOU.**

Allow me to introduce **YOU**
to your Ego and your Self.

Your Ego is your protector.

It exists to keep you safe...and alive.

It's the part of you that makes you avoid dark alleys at night. And it's also the part that keeps you from giving your boss a piece of your mind when you're pissed. Because your Ego knows that doing either of these things will put your life and/or livelihood at risk. And it can't have that. Because, in a nutshell...

Your Ego is programmed to avoid
threats and danger.

But here's the thing...your Ego thinks change = danger.

It sees change as a threat to your safety because change requires you to do things differently and venture into the unknown. And your Ego prefers to live in an environment that is familiar and predictable because it's so much easier to feel (and remain) safe there.

And that's why whenever something changes, your Ego's knee-jerk reaction is to fight and resist and kick and scream.

Its resistance may sound something like this:

> *"Are they nuts? That's never going to work."*
> *"No way! I'm not doing it / going there / using that."*
> *"I can't believe someone thought THIS was an improvement."*
> *"Hell will freeze over before I get on board with that."*

All in the name of keeping you safe.
But listen when I tell you that while your Ego is working hard to keep you safe in the familiar, easy, and known, it's also keeping you small, petty, and scared.

But the good news is…

> your Ego is not the only cook in your kitchen.

Your Self is your life force.

It exists to help you evolve, grow and expand.
It's the part of you that says:

> *"Go for the promotion!"*
> *"Run the marathon!"*
> *"Try the escargot!"*
> *"Have the difficult conversation."*
> *"Speak your truth and don't apologize for it."*

It promotes such things because your Self knows that to grow you must stretch, to learn you must fail and to get ahead you need to embrace even the scary, risky, and unknown.

Your Self is more concerned with growth than safety.

It wants you to live a full life. Not a safe one.
That's why your Self looks at change as an opportunity, not a challenge. It relishes the fact that by changing things up you could actually benefit in the end.
So when change happens, your Self might get a little hopeful.
Eager.
Dare I say, giddy.

T he Ego and the Self are the two parts of you and they balance each other out. But, as you've learned, they each see things differently, so that makes their reactions to things very different.

Try to picture the Ego on your left shoulder and the Self on the right, speaking into your opposing ears. When change happens, your Ego tries to resist that change because it could put you at risk. It tries to protect you by refusing to accept the new schedule, software, budget, etc. It crosses its arms and stubbornly says "NO!"

Meanwhile, your Self really wants you to be accepting of that change because it knows that doing so will stretch you, challenge you, educate you, evolve you. It excitedly says "YES!"

Back and forth they go.

They each have a voice, and they each want to be heard.

The problem is that our Ego has a louder voice.

Anthropologically, it had to be this way if we wanted to survive. For gabillions of years we had to look out for the saber-toothed tiger, the poisonous berry, or the opposing tribe. Threats to our survival lurked everywhere, and as a result we developed a protective, survival-based, Ego-driven default reaction.

And our constant exposure to news reports of crime, disaster, war, and other psychological stressors continues to feed the belief that danger is everywhere and it's all out to get us.
Yikes.

So it's no surprise that we all walk around with our Ego at the ready and eager to attack anything that changes. Because remember, change feels threatening.

Some of us react to even the smallest changes like they're a three-alarm fire. Few events in our lives are actually life-threatening. But we often react like they are.

Last week my manicurist told me my favorite nail polish was discontinued and, had you seen my reaction, you would've thought she told me I had a terminal illness.

My Ego has a field day with
first world problems.

But that doesn't mean I have to send my Ego packing. I just have to thoughtfully consider what events truly require an Egoic reaction and which don't.

If I had done this when Lulu told me about my nail polish, I would have seen the opportunity to try something new, like a French manicure.

Ah, the French.

When you experience an
unpleasant, unexpected,
non-life-threatening change,
which one
typically controls
your reactions,
your Ego
or
your Self?

Have you ever met people who never get flustered or bothered by anything? Some massive change comes down the pike and the most you'll get from them is an "*OK. Got it.*"

It's not that they don't have an Ego. They do. They just don't let it have as much influence, voice, and strength. They manage their Ego's voice. Resist its fear mongering. They quiet it down so they can let their Self's voice come through louder and clearer.

Like you, they have a choice.

They choose growth over complacency.

They choose action over inaction.

They choose light over dark.

They choose possibility over fear.

They choose.

And you can too.

When shift happens

and you tell your Ego to sit down

and let your Self have a say,

you are moving forward.

YES!
Forward.
That's where you're headed.

To a place where the sun
shines bright and the air
smells sweet.

A place where you can be in flow with all of the
ups and downs, ins and outs, overs and unders.

And I can help you get there with a few simple steps.

Here's how to manage that Ego of yours
and give your Self the space to create a

positive reaction

and therefore a

positive reality

when dealing with
shift.

#1 Pause

Your super-protective Ego is ready to pounce at the mere site
of a threat (or change). Give it a minute to realize there is no
bear and it will not eat your head.

#2 Ask yourself a good question

I'll show you how.

#3 Answer the question

Seriously, you have to answer it. Your Ego will try to
resist to keep you safe, small, and petty.
Give your Self the megaphone and let it sing.

Let's break these down...

#1 Pause

This step may seem over simplified, but I assure you there is nothing simple about it. Because, as you may know, there's a very complex set of neurons at work in your brain. This almond shaped mass of grey matter is called the amygdala. And that, my friend, is where your Ego lives.

Biologically speaking, when your amygdala senses danger it takes over the thinking part of your brain and sends all the oxygen to your arms and legs to prepare it to fight or flee. This leaves your brain deprived of the oxygen it needs to think clearly and make good decisions. In essence, your sweet little amygdala has the ability to take over your thinking brain and rule your reactions while ignoring logic or reason.

**This is actually an ah-mazing process
that has kept us safe and alive
for millenniums.**

Even today, if a poisonous snake jumped out of a dark alley and tried to attack you, this very system would take over, and without thinking, you would karate chop it to the throat…or run like hell.

But most events don't require such drastic reactions. Like I mentioned, most shifts aren't really that serious or life-threatening, but we can often react as if they are.

There's actually a name for this irrational overreaction to a stressful situation. It's called *amygdala hijacking,* and it's often not pretty because these reactions can lead to remorse, regret and lots of egg on your face.

When this hijacking occurs, you'll know it.

Your face may get hot and flushed, you might clench your jaw or start to feel a little shaky. Dry mouth, blurred vision, the whole bit. And in extreme cases, thoughts of punching something (or someone) pop into your head, just momentarily.

The worst though, is when YOU are the only one having this type of reaction while everyone else is just sitting there as if they can't see the "danger" that you see. And your irrational reaction to this situation triples the crazy factor for yourself.

Infuriating, I know.

You can avoid all of this with a pause.

Pause to take a deep breath, a walk, or a bath.
Pause to let the oxygen flow back to the
thinking part of your brain.
Pause to assess what type of reaction is required.
Pause to avoid boarding the train to crazy town.

Just pause.

When you want to rip someone's head off because
you're told that they're replacing your favorite
client management software, just pause.

> **When you feel like screaming** in the middle of a
> meeting about the latest budget cuts, just pause.

> > **When you want to quit** after you hear your
> > company is going through a re-org...AGAIN,
> > just pause.

By pausing, you are giving yourself a minute to consider an
alternative reaction, and therefore an alternative reality.
Pausing gives you the bandwidth you need to activate the thinking
part of your brain to explore options and avoid the fight or flight
response.

When you do this, you are literally redirecting the energy
away from the fear mongering part of your brain (Ego) and
toward the area of logic and reason (Self).

And here's what you do when you get there.

#2 Ask yourself a good question

As a professional coach, this is my go-to secret weapon to help clients move out of a mindset that keeps them stuck, and into one that moves them forward.
Check it.

Michelle comes to a coaching session stressed out about something shitty that happened at the office. Her speech is rapid-fire, she's chest breathing, and she's picking at the cuticles of *both* her thumbs. Knowing this is not her best thinking state, I listen and give her a few minutes to express and expulse, before interrupting to ask her a good question, *Michelle, what's the opportunity here?*

Right after I ask the question, I can literally watch Michelle move from one state to another. She takes a deep breath, exhales loudly, and directs her eyes upward as she begins to think about the answer.

I witness her Ego take a back seat and
her Self slip on the driving gloves.

Her shoulders soften, her fists unclench,
and her breathing begins to slow down.
By contemplating the answer, Michelle redirected her focus
away from the darkness and toward the light.
If I hadn't asked her a question (and held space for an answer)
Michelle could've continued into the downward spiral of
panicked, Ego-driven reactivity.
And who knows where that would have led her.

Michelle is so human.
And so are you.

A sking yourself a good question is the best way to shorten the distance between the moment some undesirable shift happens and the moment you get on with your life.

But mind you, not all questions are created equal. A good question will get you thinking. Because the sooner you re-direct the blood toward your rational thinking brain, the sooner you move it away from your reactive reptilian brain.

After all, you're a human, not an iguana.

So to *really* get you thinking, your questions need to be thought-provoking and purposeful. They have to be crafted in a way that serves you and your higher good.

These aren't your mother's questions. They are way, way better. And they will definitely create some good shift.

Here's how you do it…

First.
They have to be open-ended. You know, questions that can't be answered with a simple *yes* or *no*.
A good rule of thumb is to start your question with **WHAT** or **HOW**.

Next.
Research shows that we do our *best* thinking when we're asked about things that are **POSITIVE** or **DESIREABLE**.
And we are *less productive* in our thinking when we are asked about negative or undesirable stuff.

Case in point, you'd be in a much more productive state of mind if I asked you, *What do you do well?* vs. *What do you suck at?*

Sure, the latter helps you identify activities to avoid,
but it also puts you in the position to beat yourself up,
feel pathetic, and focus on errors.
This leads you into a downward spiral toward darkness.
And it's hard to find answers when it's too dark to see.
The former, however, avoids self-flogging, focuses
on your strengths, and gives you ideas to build upon.
A definite upward spiral toward the light of possibility
where you can more easily see your options.

Finally.
All you need is a little glue to stick both parts together. And said
glue is an *auxiliary verb*. Remember those?
They "help" bring it all together.
And it's extra helpful if you ask about the present or future.
So, you can choose to be your best self in the present by using:
AM/ARE/DO/DOES
or set your sites on a bright future and choose:
WILL/CAN/COULD.
Either way you slice it, you win.

Check it out...

THE GOOD QUESTION FORMULA

WHAT or HOW	+	AM/ARE/DO/DOES (present) WILL/CAN/COULD (future)	+	A POSITIVE or DESIRABLE OUTCOME
FOR EXAMPLE				
WHAT	+	**CAN** I	+	**APPRECIATE** ABOUT THIS?
HOW	+	**DOES** THIS	+	**HELP** ME?

So simple, right?

Now, notice, you can't ignore or leave out any of the three parts. For example, you can't ask *Does this help me?* because that doesn't get you thinking enough and it's too easy to answer with *No, it doesn't.*
Better to ask *How does this help me?* This is assumptive in nature and gets you thinking harder about the specifics.

Hence, a good question.

You also want to avoid asking questions that could get you down in the dumps like, *What do I hate about this?*
Better to ask *What can I appreciate about this?*
Now that's a good question that can open up the blinds and let the sunshine in.

Sure, there are a bunch of other formulas and ways to craft questions, but I recommend you start here.
'Start' being the operative word.

You have to start doing this
for it to work.

Or don't start. It's your choice.

You can keep walking about the world letting your Ego run the show even when its services are not required. Or you can pause, ask yourself a question and let your Self do its thing.

But when you do decide to start, know that it will be challenging at first. You're not used to doing things this way. Your Ego may have been singing its tune for decades, but if you pass the mic to your Self and let it sing like Sinatra, it'll feel like the summer wind, came blowin' in from across the sea.

I promise.

Meanwhile. here's a little crib sheet...

THE GOOD QUESTION FORMULA

WHAT or HOW	+	AM/ARE/DO/DOES (present) WILL/CAN/COULD (future)	+	A POSITIVE or DESIRABLE OUTCOME

WHAT	HOW
What can I be **grateful** for?	How could this **benefit** me?
What am I willing to **let go** of?	How can I turn this into an **opportunity**?
What could I **learn** from this?	How will I be a **good role model** for others?
What will this **help** me do or be?	How will I **make this work** for me?
What do I need to **move beyond** this?	How will I proceed with **grace and class**?
What can I actually **control** here?	How do I **deserve** to feel?
What will I do to **make the most** of this?	How can I **improve** this situation?
What are my **options**?	How do I **want** to show up right now?

These are good questions.

Good questions create **Good shift.**

These questions will help you deal with
shift by shifting your perspective.

They help you control your reactions
before your reactions control you.

They help you
take your power back.

They help you control
the outcome of your life.

But they can't do it alone.

You have to…

#3 Answer the question

I know, more work.

But you're only halfway to controlville if you just ask yourself a question. The magic happens when you answer it because it

completes the circle,

closes the gap,

clears the clouds,

and makes the sun come out.

Now, your Ego will fight this because even contemplating a question takes you out of the protective fight or flight state where you can be on your guard.

Your Ego will also resist answering the question in a positive way because this could also put you in harm's way. For example, in answer to that question, *How does this help me?* Your Ego will want to reply with *It doesn't!* And that's fine. It's just doing its job to keep you safe (and small).

But your Self has a different perspective to bring. Remember, your Self wants to stretch and grow and learn. And if you want that for your Self then give it the mic.

Now, in the moment of choosing which part to listen to, pay attention. You will feel the Ego and the Self fighting for the right to party. But remember, you have a choice.

When you choose to answer the question, and you choose to answer it in a positive way, your Self is winning the fight and you are on your way to an outcome free of regrets, full of control and lots of personal growth.

Let me show you how this might play out.

THE SHIFT:
You've been informed that the report you're working on
needs to be delivered sooner than originally expected.
This means you'll have to work overtime to get it done.

#1 PAUSE: Breathe/pray/take a walk

#2 ASK: How can I turn this into an opportunity?

#3 ANSWER: *I will use this as an opportunity to show*
everyone how well I perform under pressure.

THE OUTCOME:
Your boss recognizes you at the company retreat as a fear-
less, kung-fu master of deadly deadlines.

****

THE SHIFT:
You learn that your job is on the chopping block as the
company starts to downsize.

#1 PAUSE: Breathe/smile/hum a tune

#2 ASK: How can this benefit me?

#3 ANSWER: *Maybe I could finally start that boutique land-*
scaping business I've been talking about.

THE OUTCOME:
You avoid the stress and headache that often comes with
being downsized and seek greener pastures.

THE SHIFT:
You learn that a long-time client has chosen to go with another vendor.

#1 PAUSE: Breathe/count to ten/sing a song

#2 ASK: What could I learn from this?

#3 ANSWER: *I could learn what I could have done to keep their business.*

THE OUTCOME:
You ask. They tell you. You promise to do it and they agree to keep you on.

Now you...

****

THE SHIFT: Your colleague of seven years got a promotion and is now your manager.

#1 PAUSE :

#2 ASK:

#3 ANSWER:

THE OUTCOME:

Easy breezy, right?

Now here's a small but important caveat…
You can learn this and practice pausing, asking questions, and answering them all day long, but as I mentioned earlier, it may not just magically fall into place overnight.

This is a new approach. It may be quite different than what you've been doing, and some part of you will find it uncomfortable, namely your Ego, who's been driving the bus for a while. So it's gonna take some time, practice, and patience to ease it out of the driver's seat.

The best way to do this is to simply observe your Ego.
Be a student of it. Try to understand its patterns and fears.
And by all means, be kind to it and appreciate it for protecting you and keeping you safe all these years.

Then, tell it to sit its ass down until you call its name.

Here's how it might sound…

"Dearest Ego, I so appreciate you for watching out for me and doing your best to keep me from stretching my Self too much. I understand that you're doing this out of pure kindness, love, and a desire to keep me safe. Honestly, I don't know what I'd do without you. You've helped me avoid some serious risks...like that time I got drunk at the office holiday party and wanted to dance on the bar. What a good pal you were that night.

Anyway, I've been noticing that sometimes you can overstep your boundaries and try to protect me from things that I really don't need help with...like that time that I got pissed at Lisa for taking the lead on MY project. I definitely didn't need to react that way. My thumb still hurts a little bit.

So, as much as I appreciate your good intentions, I need you to back it up a bit. Not completely, because I still need you around for some serious stuff. But I'm gonna ask you to keep a lid on it when little shifts happen that really aren't a huge threat...like the account I lost last week. I know you want to blame Kevin for blowing the deal and it would be fun to be passive aggressive to him the next time he tries to "help me" but that's starting to feel petty. And the truth is, I've been reading this great book and I'm realizing that reacting that way takes up a lot of my emotional bandwidth, energy and power that I could be using elsewhere.

It sucks, I know. I too will miss our mini spaz attacks because that little surge of adrenaline is yummy. But I can't keep chasing the dragon, little buddy. I've gotta move on. And I have to ask you to just step in when absolutely necessary...like at the wedding I'll be attending this weekend. I'll be drinking...so, um, yeah."

REFLECTION QUESTIONS

When does your Ego tend to react out of fear?

What is it trying to protect you from?

How would your Self like to react?

What will your go-to question be when shift happens?

Again, this is gonna take a while, so buckle up and enjoy the ride.
I've been at this shift for years and when I find my Ego creeping
out of its little hole, sometimes I whack it like a mole.
Other times I get lazy and indulge in its antics.
And you'll do the same.
But keep at it and you'll get better at this little game.
That's life, isn't it?
It's just a game, and you get to play it any way you want.
Whack. Be whacked. Be a whacko.
It's your choice.

SHARE THE SHIFT

I f you're like most, you probably have a list of people who could really use this stuff. The over-reactors, negative naysayers and complainers in your life who make everyone in their wake pay for their misery.

And as you're reading, you may be thinking, *Man, if I could just get so-and-so to read this book!* Or *If what's-her-name could apply some of this, my life would be so much better.*

You can't help it.
You're seeing the power in this and you want to bestow it on the energy-sucking black holes in your life.
I get it.

Sure you can tell people how they might react in a different way to get a different result. Tell them they are not a victim and that the words they choose make up the fabric of their life. At the very least you could remind them they always have a choice.

Or, you could just ask them a question.

Yep. The Good Question Formula can be used to create shift-worthy questions that you can ask others. You know, those people who love to come to you to complain about this shift or the other. Or those victim-y types that love to play the blame game. You now have a tool to help them help themselves.

You're welcome.

H ere are a few guidelines to set you (and them) up for success:

- Remember, it's not enough to just ask them a question. They must ANSWER THE QUESTION.

- Leave lots of space for the answer to emerge. Silence is key, so try to get comfortable with it.

- Don't let your question trail off with some rhetorical sounding tone. It's a real question so let them know you expect a real answer.

- Expect them to resist answering. Because they will. It's just their Ego trying to keep them small, petty, and safe. But you know better.

Just hold the space for them, sit back and watch the magic unfold.

- Help your question land better by prefacing it with a supportive statement that helps them feel seen and heard.

- Resist answering the question for them. It's always more powerful when the answer comes from them.

Here's how you might look in action…

MIKE: Ughhh! This is so stupid! I can't believe they expect us to learn a new computer system and they're not even training us on it.

YOU: Wow, it sounds like you're really upset about this. Let me ask you a question, what can you do to become more familiar with the system?

■■■

LAURA: I've had my own private office for three years and now you expect me to move to an open cubicle?

YOU: I can understand this is difficult for you, Laura. Let me ask you this, what are some benefits of working in an open cubicle?

■■■

PAT: With the changes from this new legislation we are actually more restricted in how we can help our clients!

YOU: I can really relate to your frustration and I'm curious, how could you turn this into an opportunity?

Ask questions like these often enough and I guarantee Mike, Laura and Pat will find somewhere else to air their grievances.

Again, you're welcome.

N ow you're thinking, that's all well and good, but what if they refuse to answer the question?

Give a shift. But just one.

When you offer up a powerful question, and with it an opportunity to see shift differently, observe their response to your generous gift. If they are receptive and eager to grow, they will answer the question.

If not, back off.

You can't force people to jump on your gravy train. If they're not ready, you can't *make* them handle shift with the same grace and thoughtfulness as you.

If you're surrounded by people who live in a negative space, let them own it as *theirs* not *yours*. Allow them to be where they are and don't agree to join them.

Honoring people where they are is the best gift you can give them — just insist on receiving the same respect from them.

And along the way, remember that your job is not to change or control ANYBODY. Your job is to choose a reaction that gives you the reality you want.

And that includes how you react to
people who don't want to shift.

THE
GOOD
SHIFT

Are you by chance
familiar with Babushka Dolls?
They're beautiful Russian dolls of
decreasing size stacked one inside another.
Well, you've got the equivalent of one
right here and it's gonna lead you to your
biggest choice of all. The choice within the
choice. And it goes like this...
You know that shift always happens.
And when shift happens you have a choice.

You know the choices you can make.

You have tools to help you make those choices.

You have tools to help *others* make those choices.

But the mother lode of all choices is whether you

choose to make any of these choices. I mean, just

because you now know all of this doesn't mean

you have to go out and do anything with it.

Remember, you always have a choice. You are free to
ignore this and go through life any way you choose.
But what will happen if you choose to apply this stuff?
Why stretch yourself to exercise your power of choice?
What is the payoff for going through the trouble?
Oh, I am sooooo glad you asked.

When you choose to exercise
your power of choice
you are free.

Free from the prison of victimhood.
Free from pain and suffering.
Free from fear.
Free from confusion, indecision, and regret.
Free from the epidemic of a scarcity mentality.
Free from self-doubt, blame, and judgment.

And with that comes the freedom to
live the life you desire.
The freedom to play a bigger game.
You are free to succeed at anything.
Free to find ease, flow, peace, and joy
wherever you look.
Simply because you choose to.

When shift happens and you effectively choose
   who you are,
      what you say, and
         how you react,
            you are choosing to
               be in flow.

Being in flow looks like a leaf floating downstream *with* the current, versus a salmon swimming upstream *against* the current.

Being in *flow* with change frees up
all the energy you would be using
to *resist* change.

And you can channel that energy
   toward more
      productive efforts
         like holding onto your power
            and designing your destiny.

What's more (as if you need more),
being in flow will positively affect you
emotionally, physically, socially and professionally.

Emotionally. You won't be that crabby apple because you choose your feelings instead of letting *them* choose *you* based on circumstances that are out of your control.
You stop blaming others for making you feel sad, mad, or bad. And you use words that support you in getting what you want, which puts you in the driver's seat winning the race.

Physically. You don't need a doctor to tell you that being less irritable, angry, resentful, and stressed out about shift is bad for your health. Taking control of your reactions means taking control of your health. Bam. Power move. Take that, beta blockers.

Socially. No one wants to hang out and drink beers with a Negative Nancy who plays small, acts like a victim and drowns their misery in Budweiser. No. People like the positive, happily buzzed version of you that's drunk on life because you own your power and stand in it every day.

Professionally. You will be a rockstar. Not only will you be modeling behavior you hope to see in others, but people will be attracted to you like mosquitoes to a bug light. Managing your Ego and asking yourself and others really good questions will most certainly earn you Employee of the Year...or month.
Either way, congrats.

T hat's the really good shift you get to experience when you choose to be the super hero that you are.

Showing up every day making choices
that serve you.

Choices that lift you up not bring you down.
Choices that keep you from getting stuck in the muck.
Choices that make you feel more alive.

You deserve to feel alive.
You deserve to be the best version of yourself.
You deserve to live your best life, emotionally, physically, socially, and professionally.

All of those things are possible and very much
within
your
control.

All you have to do is choose.

REMEMBER

You always have a choice.
And nobody, nowhere,
no how, can ever take
THAT away from

YOU.

REFLECTION QUESTIONS

How does it feel to have so many choices?

How will your life be different as a result of reading this book?

How will your work be different?

What are you going to do now?

Who do you want to be?

The last two are biggies, so you may need
to sit with them for a minute.

What you do now and who you choose to be
are powerful beginnings to the story
you will start writing today.
The curtain's up, stage lights are on
and you're the star of the show, the writer and director.
And as you know, your story has a limited number of acts left,
so make the most of the time you have.

I'll be right here cheering you on
because you are one cool cat
and I'm your biggest fan.

Congrats on finishing the book.

That tells me you're committed.
Committed to dealing with change before it deals with you.
Committed to holding on to your power.
Committed to living a fuller life
in which you not only survive but thrive.
I believe in your ability to do ALL of those things and
I want to support you along the way.

Head over to my website to find additional resources.
www.jenniferpowers.com
While you're there, drop me a line to tell me about the
awesome choices you're making and the results you're getting.

Until then, stay amazing.

Believing in you,

Jennifer

Too good to keep to yourself?

Get a copy for each team member, department, or your entire organization.

Email info@jenniferpowers.com for bulk discounts on stacks of *Good shift!*

Want the real deal?
Hire Jen to speak.

Over 300,000 people across the world have experienced Jennifer's lively, interactive keynotes. Delivering her powerful message with wit and energy, she lights up the room and leaves a lasting impact.

If you liked *Good shift!* you're gonna love the book that started it all.

Jennifer's best-selling book *Oh, shift!* has helped people all over the world create positive shifts in their personal lives that improved their work, health, relationships, finances, and overall perspective.
You deserve some of that shift.

Get all of this and more at www.jenniferpowers.com

P.S. You are good.
Real good. xo

WHAT PEOPLE ARE SAYING ABOUT *POWER FOR LIFE* . . .

"Because Pastor Jeff Leake actually lives and breathes the book of Acts and is planting life-giving churches, the book you are holding in your hands is explosive. This isn't just a collection of eloquent and wise words, but a book that has the demonstrative and life-transforming power of the Jesus gospel on every page. This is more than just 'desk or university knowledge' by a professor, but well-tested and proven teaching from discipleship training and the frontier of evangelism. Read it, teach it, and see how the Holy Spirit will transform lives."

—*Johannes Amritzer, founder and president, Mission SOS International; author of* How Jesus Healed the Sick and You Can Too

"We live in a world desperately in need of Spirit-baptized, Spirit-filled, and Spirit-empowered people. In his book *Power for Life* Jeff Leake provides a Bible-saturated tour of the life every Christian should long for and experience. Read this book expecting your life to change!"

—*John Lindell, lead pastor, James River Church, Springfield, MO*

"Jeff has written another devotional book that has the potential to change your Christian walk dramatically. Get your hands on this book and grow spiritually."

—*Rob Ketterling, lead pastor, River Valley Church, Apple Valley, MN*

"I have met many world leaders, professional athletes, and successful business people, yet Jeff Leake always stands out to me as one of the finest men I have been privileged to know. He doesn't encourage others to walk where he has not walked himself. *Power for Life* is a guidebook to a deeper walk with the Holy Spirit, and it is as authentic as Jeff himself."

—*Stephen J. Avery, former Pittsburg Steeler, Avery Family Ministries, Pittsburg, PA*

"In this book, *Power for Life*, Jeff uses compelling biblical events and dramatic personal accounts to prove the power of the Holy Spirit can and still does make a difference in the lives of believers today. The Holy Spirit is God adding His super to our natural."

—*James Leake, president, Acts 20:24 Ministries*

"Few issues are as important to Pentecostals as their personal experience in the life of the Spirit. There are also few issues that are as confusing to non-Pentecostals as this same experience. Jeff approaches this subject in a thoughtful, biblical, and experiential way that I'm confident will remove much confusion and add much clarity to the importance of a dynamic Spirit-filled life for all believers. I would encourage individual and group study of this work with the anticipation of a greater power for service for our Lord."

—*Stephen R. Tourville, superintendent, PennDel Network of the Assemblies of God; co-author,* Better Together: Harnessing the Power of Teamwork

"Pastor Jeff Leake writes a practical, eye-opening guide to accessing the supernatural power of the Holy Spirit. It's hard to imagine a more challenging and liberating exploration of this surprisingly unexplored area—the crucial role of the Holy Spirit in the lives of believers. *Power for Life* will bring you face-to-face with the limitless potential God has for you."

—*Brian Bolt; founder, CityReach Network; lead pastor, CityReach Church Pittsburgh, PA; author,* Reach: A Story of Multiplication in the City

"With the privilege of knowing Jeff personally, I have witnessed the power of miracles at work in his life's journey. *Power for Life* is a great bridge for conversation to discuss the supernatural reality of the life-changing experience of the baptism in the Holy Spirit. You will enjoy the story-strengthened, practical approach that gives anyone food for thought and opens the dialogue for interaction. As you read, enjoy your personal journey for the miracle God has in store for you."

—*Ron Heitman, lead pastor, Evangel Church, Hanover Park, IL*

"I stand in awe of the simplicity, biblical integrity, and practicality of this book. Without a doubt you are about to read one of the best books on the Holy Spirit; it is able to catapult any believer into a fruitful and adventurous Christian journey."

—*Fernando DeCarvalho, executive director, SOS Adventure Office*

"I have been a pastor for over thirteen years and experienced the baptism in the Holy Spirit for the first time this past year at Jeff's church. As evidenced in this book, Jeff has a unique ability to make this beautiful and exciting

Christian experience understandable and accessible to many Christians. I pray God will use this book to take everyday believers to new levels of worship, prayer, and service—to release a river of fervency from within every soul that encounters it."

—*Dr. Dan Muttart, Pittsburgh PA*

"Nothing will ignite your faith like the power of the Holy Spirit! And nothing will ignite your hunger like real-life stories. *Power for Life* will leave you longing and looking for your own book of Acts experience!"

—*Ron Johnson, pastor, One Church, Orlando, FL*

"I grew up in churches that were alive with the tangible power of the Holy Spirit, and I'm eager to reproduce those experiences in our church today. I'm also eager to do it in a way that's sensitive to the seekers in our city who are exploring faith and giving church a shot. Jeff Leake has taught me how to introduce people to the transcendent presence of the Holy Spirit without being weird. This book is a gift for anyone who wants to experience the fullness of the Spirit in a culturally sensitive way."

—*Brad Leach, lead pastor, CityLife Church, Philadelphia, PA*

"When I first heard that Jeff Leake was writing a book on the baptism in the Holy Spirit I immediately said to myself, 'Finally!' and for this simple reason: Jeff has an incredible gift to preach and teach on any given topic and make it easy to understand and apply. And since the book is about my favorite topic, I couldn't be happier! On every single page of this book Jeff makes you long for the power of the Holy Spirit over your life and for the ability to live a 'book of Acts' lifestyle each day. Not only that but he stirs up the faith in you that it is possible! I can't wait to see how many lives will be changed forever by reading *Power for Life!*"

—*Samuel Strandberg, executive director, Northeast Ministry School*

"In *Power for Life*, author Jeff Leake helps us take that beautiful, biblical, but often under-accessed, gift of the baptism in the Holy Spirit off the shelf. In a clear, compelling way (and with life-in-the-real-world stories), Jeff removes the wrappings of confusion and controversy (maybe even—dare I say it?—weirdness) to reveal the one thing our weak hearts have been longing for all along: Holy Spirit power to live the vivid Jesus-is-alive message in this broken world.

Maybe the idea of Spirit baptism is brand-new to you. Or perhaps, like me, you need fresh eyes to see the vast potential for empowering transformation available to every believer through this gift from Jesus. Either way, *Power for Life* is for you. And by the way. . . that's not just a statement about the title: power for life is for you!"

—*Jodi Detrick, religion columnist for* The Seattle Times, *author of* The Jesus-Hearted Woman

"I absolutely love this new book. Not only do I 100 percent believe in what Jeff is sharing, I'm ecstatic that a contemporary leader and pastor has written a new book on the baptism in the Holy Spirit. The storytelling, theology, passion, quotes, and the practical path Jeff lays out for anyone to receive the baptism in the Holy Spirit will make *Power for Life* an important book for many years to come. I plan on distributing it widely and promoting it enthusiastically because every Christian needs to read it."

— *Scott Hagan, president, North Central University, Minneapolis, MN*

"Jeff Leake is an incredible communicator. He takes eternal truths and makes them accessible through practical insight and inspiring stories, always painting a clear path to personal transformation. But what really adds weight to what any author or communicator has to say is that person's testimony and spiritual fruit—and when you appraise Jeff's life, you see that he has fruit and lots of it. I wholeheartedly recommend *Power for Life* because of the powerful truths clearly articulated that impart faith for Holy Spirit impact in your life and ministry. Get ready for God to add new chapters to your story as you experience His power for life."

—*Justin Maslanka, lead pastor, CityReach Church, Cleveland, OH*

POWER
FOR LIFE

WHY EVERY BELIEVER NEEDS TO BE BAPTIZED
IN THE HOLY SPIRIT

JEFF LEAKE

Gospel Publishing House

Published by Gospel Publishing House
1445 N. Boonville Ave.
Springfield, Missouri 65802

www.myhealthychurch.com

Cover and interior design and formatting by Prodigy Pixel
(www.prodigypixel.com)

02-4221

ISBN: 978-1-60731-468-4

Printed in the United States of America

21 20 19 18 17 ● 2 3 4 5 6

This book is dedicated to my parents, James and Rebecca Leake, who modeled for me so many things.

First of all, they allowed me to process all of my doubts and questions about the things of God without ever being threatened. They patiently answered me and let me struggle with my doubts and hesitations about how the Holy Spirit works.

Second, they demonstrated for me a humble heart of love and service for people.

Third, they live a life marked by the power of God. I grew up hearing stories of God's healing power at work in peoples' lives as a specific result of my father's prayers.

Finally, my parents demonstrated to me faithfulness to each other for over fifty years, and to the local church they pastored for forty years. I will be forever thankful for your role in my life.

CONTENTS

FOREWORD

Here is who should read this dynamic book, *Power for Life*, written by my friend Jeff Leake:

You, if you are hungry for a deeper walk with Jesus. He promised He would send the Holy Spirit and He has—but, not just historically. He has sent the Holy Spirit as a gift to you. This book will help you know how to experience the baptism in the Holy Spirit.

You, if you want to know more about the baptism in the Holy Spirit, speaking in other tongues, and how to receive that baptism as a gift.

You, if you aren't aware of or are confused about speaking in other tongues. Not only will you learn the scriptural teaching about speaking in other tongues, you will encounter the life experiences of those who have and the dramatic changes in their lives as a result.

You, if at one time you experienced the baptism in the Holy Spirit but lately find your life doesn't seem to be one that is filled with the Spirit. *Power for Life* will help generate a new hunger in you for an up-to-date experience with the Holy Spirit.

You, if you are a pastor or teacher who has shied away from teaching about the baptism in the Holy Spirit because you worry that such teaching will scare people away from your church or ministry. People are actually hungry to experience the supernatural. The contents of *Power for Life* will put courage back into your preaching and teaching to declare what the Word of God says about the baptism in the Holy Spirit and speaking in a language you did not learn. Make this book into a sermon or teaching series and provide a copy to every member of your church or group.

Remember that all the authors of the New Testament were baptized in the Holy Spirit and spoke in other tongues. On the Day of Pentecost, when the baptism in the Holy Spirit first happened to 120 believers who spoke in other tongues, Peter declared that the promise of this experience was for "you and your children and for all who are far off" (Acts 2:39). Notice the word *all*! That means you are included!

Open your mind, your heart, and your spirit as you read *Power for Life*. The Holy Spirit wants to give you that power. It's His gift to you. Let Jeff Leake pour into your life encouragement drawn from sound scriptural teaching, his personal journey, and the experiences of others whose lives have been transformed by the power and blessing of the Holy Spirit.

This isn't a hard book to read. It isn't technical. But, it's real. It tells you exactly what the Bible teaches about the baptism in the Holy Spirit and speaking with other tongues, and wonderfully illustrates the power of this experience in the lives of all who receive this gift from God. This book will also give you practical guidance for how you can receive power for life.

Every follower of Jesus should read this book, as well as those who are on the journey to experience Jesus.

—Dr. George O. Wood, general superintendent, The General Council of the Assemblies of God

INTRODUCTION

When I sat down to write about this topic, I was amazed just how little has been written over the years about the baptism in the Holy Spirit. Especially since entire denominations and church movements have been shaped by this experience. Yet, so few have attempted to explain the practical value and biblical reasoning behind this important moment in a believer's spiritual journey.

People may avoid this topic for several reasons. First of all, *it's controversial.* There are so many strong feelings about when the baptism in the Holy Spirit occurs in the life of the believer, how it happens, and what evidence demonstrates that it has happened in a person's life. For some it has become a dividing line, of sorts, for defining fellowship. Meaning that if you don't agree with my position on the matter . . . I don't want to have anything to do with you.

In my opinion, that kind of attitude is not only unbiblical, it's downright silly.

We need to leave room for others to disagree with us. Our choice of who we love, do life with, and minister beside should never be completely defined by variances of opinion on matters like this. We have to be bigger and better than that. Yet, we don't enrich true fellowship when we avoid a controversial subject. I always learn from those with whom I disagree. My hope is that this book will be a source of good discussion and interaction, regardless of whether or not you agree with everything written here.

The second reason people avoid this topic has to do with both *awkwardness* and *confusion.* Maybe for you, the last few paragraphs meant absolutely nothing. Not only are you unaware of any controversy, you are not at all familiar with the experience. The biggest reaction from those who are new to the concept of the baptism in the Holy Spirit happens when they hear the phrase "speaking in tongues." The blank looks on their faces and their question "What are you even talking about?" say it all.

Those who do know the meaning of the term *tongues* often aren't sure how to explain it to someone who is asking questions. What they have experienced personally might even confuse their thinking. So there's an inevitable sense of awkwardness whenever the topic comes up.

A few months ago, I was standing in line at a coffee shop that I frequent regularly. The barista girls there know that I'm a pastor. So when I come into the store, they greet me, "Hey, Pastor Jeff,'" which is always funny because the entire room turns to see the "holy man" who just entered the coffee shop. Well, on this particular morning, one of the girls added something to the greeting. "Hey, Pastor Jeff, we were waiting for you because we have a question. What is this deal about 'speaking in tongues'?"

Talk about being put on the spot!

As far as I know, none of these barista girls are believers. They asked this question, loudly, in front of a full store.(It was around 6:45 a.m., and the line to get coffee was long.) I had thirty seconds to answer while they filled my order for a Grande Dark Roast. What in the world do I even say in such a short time and in a public forum?

Here's what I said, "We believe God does miracles, which are events that can't be explained as natural phenomenon. Do you believe that?" I asked them. "Yes, I believe God can do miracles," each replied. I looked around to see everyone around me, in line, leaning in and nodding their heads. Then I added, "Speaking in tongues is just a miracle of language. God prompts a person to speak a language they have never learned as a sign that He is at work in a situation. I know that sounds kind of out there, but you can imagine if someone spoke to you in English and they had never studied it, that would be a pretty convincing sign that God was talking to you."

They all laughed, nodded their heads at my explanation, and

seemed satisfied. I could tell that was all they were ready to hear at the moment. So I picked up my Grande and sat down in my normal seat and sipped my coffee.

I have found that many people are curious and yet confused about this subject. Well, the baptism in the Holy Spirit involves a discussion about "speaking in tongues," but it involves so much more than that. In fact, the baptism in the Holy Spirit is truly the gateway to living a supernatural life. God is a God of miracles. He wants to do miracles in and through each of our lives.

That's why this topic is so important. But the controversy and the sense of awkward confusion seem to prevent us from having an open and intentional discussion of how to be true to ourselves and yet how to live a supernatural life. I have had so many conversations with young church leaders who have serious questions not only about the biblical nature of this experience, but also about the practical value of it. The questions they have are, "What does it do? Why is it necessary? And why can't we have a serious dialogue about this and about how it fits into our lives and ministries?"

I want to get the dialogue started. I also want to teach how this experience is so valuable for every believer. My passion is to see every person who believes in Jesus come to an understanding of how God can use them to experience miracles. I want every believer to understand who they are in Christ and who the Holy Spirit is within their lives. Too many believers are living out of their own strength and wisdom. They don't understand who lives within them and what He is capable of doing for and through them.

As you read this book, don't read it to resolve a controversy or solve some sense of awkward confusion. Read this book to come to grips with the supernatural potential within your life. Read it with a hunger to see God do all He is able to do through your life. Read it with an open mind to discover things about your mission as a person that you may never have known before. As you read this book, hopefully you will pick up on three things regarding my writing/teaching style:

It's Scripture-based: My goal is to base every principle in every chapter on something the Bible teaches. We can discover so much about the baptism in the Holy Spirit in the New Testament. My desire is to write accurately and practically about what the Bible clearly declares we can expect and believe.

It's story-oriented: I learn best through the lives of others. So when I consider a biblical concept, I want to see how that concept expresses itself in the real world and in the lives of normal people. So in each chapter I tell at least one story about how the baptism in the Holy Spirit has made an impact on someone's life in a powerful way.

It's simple: I'm not a complicated thinker. Yes, I can hold a discussion about deep theological truths with those who want to dive into the more profound and precise aspects of theological interpretation, but my gift is to take what is complicated and explain it in the simplest of terms so that everyone can understand and apply what is written.

If you're looking for an overtly theological treatment of the subject, this isn't the book that will accomplish that goal. This book is for people who know little or nothing about the baptism in the Holy Spirit; yet it's also for those who want to look at the subject in a fresh way. It's designed to be practical and motivational.

I hope that once you have read this book you'll have had a personal experience with God. You'll have a greater understanding of your Best Friend, the Holy Spirit, you'll see the potential for God to work through your life to release supernatural things into your world, and you'll be able to explain what you have experienced based on Bible passages that address this work of God.

May you be blessed as you begin this journey.

CHAPTER ONE

IT'S MORE THAN ENOUGH!

Take the Holy Spirit out of the equation of my life, and it would spell
b-o-r-i-n-g. Add him to the equation of your life, and anything can happen.[1]

—MARK BATTERSON

What we have without the baptism in the Holy Spirit is simply not enough!

This is the conclusion Jesus' disciples would have reached when they heard Him make this statement: "Do not leave Jerusalem, but wait for the gift my Father promised, which you have heard me speak about. For John baptized with water, but in a few days you will be baptized with the Holy Spirit" (Acts 1:4–5). Consider the whirlwind of change that Peter, James, John and the others had just been through.

Only weeks earlier, they had watched their leader as He was nailed to the cross. For three years, they had followed this revolutionary leader, Jesus of Nazareth. While Jesus had predicted the moment of His death, biblical history reveals that the disciples were personally and emotionally unprepared to face it. Their Messiah was crucified. He died. Friends took His body down from the cross and buried Him in a tomb.

All seemed hopeless. Nothing made sense. The disciples hid away, afraid that their own lives were in danger.

Then came Sunday!

Jesus rose. The stone was rolled away. The dead body of their Master came back to life, and they saw Him in His resurrected form. Talk about a game-changer! If this was possible, then anything was possible! People don't just come back from the dead! But Jesus did. He conquered death. He overcame the grave, and in so doing He proved that He was who He said He was.

> God knows you aren't adequate for the task *in your own strength*.

Acts 1:3 tells us, "After his suffering, he presented himself to them [the disciples] and gave many convincing proofs that he was alive. He appeared to them over a period of forty days and spoke about the kingdom of God." During this forty-day period of time, Jesus began to unfold to His disciples what He wanted them to do next. His mission for them, should they accept it, was to take the message of His resurrection to the entire planet. Every person, every race, every nation was not only to hear about what had happened but was to be invited into a personal relationship with God through Jesus Christ: "Go and make disciples of all nations, baptizing them in the name of the Father and of the Son and of the Holy Spirit, and teaching them to obey everything I have commanded you" (Matthew 28:19–20).

Can you imagine? If you have listened to teachings from the Bible, you have probably heard these famous verses. The challenge Jesus gave to His disciples is often referred to as the Great Commission. But when you think of the implications of this commission it seems to be more like a *huge impossibility*.

- Most of these disciples weren't formally educated.
- Many of them were in their early twenties—some in their late teens.
- All of them lived in a very poor region under the domination of Roman rule.
- For most of the three years they had walked with Jesus, the twelve disciples hadn't gotten along very well.

- Several of them were rivals and were battling for top position in this discipleship group.
- None of them had traveled more than a few hundred miles from home.
- All this took place in an era of limited technology. Travel was by horse or by foot. There were no phones, tweets, emails, or even an established pony express.

Now Jesus expected them to take over the world!

By the way, we should mention that He wanted them to do all of this *without Him*. Just after He gave this commission, He disappeared. "After he said this, he was taken up before their very eyes, and a cloud hid him from their sight" (Acts 1:9).

What we have in our lives without the power of the Holy Spirit is simply *not enough*!

Can you identify with that reality? Everyone of us faces things in our lives that cause us to admit, "What I have right now is simply not enough!"

- Addictions we have tried and tried to overcome
- Depressing circumstances that constantly drag us down
- Complications with our family relationships that leave us frustrated and confused
- Habits we just can't seem to break
- Needs we just can't meet
- Visions and dreams we want to pursue but can't see how they'll become a reality

Even our attempts to follow Christ faithfully often feel hollow and lacking; we feel like we don't measure up. We slot the life we want to live into the "huge impossibility" category and feel powerless and inadequate to do anything about it.

If you have felt that way, I have some really good news for you: God knows you aren't adequate for the task *in your own strength*. Your inadequacy doesn't surprise Him. It doesn't shake His confidence in you or in His plans for your life. It doesn't limit what He can do in and through you.

In fact, becoming aware of our own personal inadequacy *must* happen before God can do powerful things in our lives. Jesus taught this principle in His famous Sermon on the Mount: "Blessed are the poor in spirit, for theirs is the kingdom of heaven" (Matthew 5:3). We could paraphrase that statement like this: Nothing changes in my life until I'm willing to admit that I need help.

Before we go on in this chapter, why don't you stop and read that last sentence out loud to yourself. How did you feel? Do you agree with what you said? Did you resist this thought? It's critically important that we accept this truth before we can move forward to make changes in our lives.

You must recognize your need for something more before God can release something amazing in and through your life. Self-dependency is the enemy of a supernatural life, the life God has in mind for you. Think about that word *supernatural*. It means "above and beyond what is naturally possible." It involves accessing a power that is not within our natural selves. It describes what happens when God gets involved with people who are willing to trust Him.

THE POWER OF THE HOLY SPIRIT CHANGED PETER'S LIFE

Consider Simon Peter, one of the disciples. He was part of the inner circle of Jesus' discipleship group. There were twelve disciples, and Jesus spent the most time with three of them: Peter, James, and John. Peter's life serves as a picture of what God wants to do in our lives.

1. *Peter tried to serve God in his own strength.*
There's probably no better moment that defines Simon Peter than the moment he promised Jesus undying loyalty. It was just after the Last Supper. Jesus had predicted that He would be betrayed and

that everyone in the room would forsake Him at His moment of greatest need. Simon Peter spoke up with all the self-confidence he could muster: "Even if all fall away on account of you, I never will" (Matthew 26:33). And again he pledged, "Even if I have to die with you, I will never disown you" (Matthew 26:35).

When Simon Peter made these promises to Jesus, I believe he was serious. He truly meant to follow through, but he had no idea how weak he actually was and how strong his desire for self-preservation would be. When the moment of truth came, Peter denied even knowing Jesus, not once but three times.

2. Peter was inconsistent in his efforts, at best.
This wasn't the first time Simon Peter had demonstrated his good intentions and inconsistent results.

- One minute he was walking on the water with Jesus; the next moment he was sinking in the waves, overwhelmed by fear.
- One minute he was making the greatest confession ever (that Jesus is the Son of God); the next minute he was rebuking Jesus to His face for even considering the mission of dying on the cross.
- One minute he was standing boldly in the garden of Gethsemane, sword in hand, attacking the men trying to arrest Jesus. The next minute, he was calling curses down on himself while he denied ever knowing Jesus.

Don't you just love this guy! I appreciate Simon Peter because I see so much of myself in him. He meant well. He even did well from time to time. But then his own sinful, selfish nature took over and he couldn't sustain the forward momentum in his life.

3. Eventually, Peter failed miserably and despaired of life.
The Bible tells us that when Simon Peter uttered his third denial, a rooster crowed. It was just as Jesus had predicted. "This very night, before

the rooster crows, you will disown me three times" (Matthew 26:34).

What a terrible moment! Can you see it? Peter insisted to the servant girl who inquired of his connection to Christ, "I swear to you, I don't know the man!" Right at that moment, as the dawn was ready to break, the rooster cried out. Peter looked up, remembering what Jesus had predicted. He glanced over to where Jesus was on trial for His life. There, Peter's eyes met the eyes of his friend and master. What deep sadness he must have seen in Jesus' eyes. Luke 22:62 tells us that Simon Peter "went outside and wept bitterly."

> Coming face-to-face with our own selfishness and sinfulness is life-altering, but it's a necessary step to be used by God.

Have you been there? Face to face with your own failure? Overcome by the sorrow of your own selfish behavior? Despairing of life because you see the despicable nature of your own heart?

Simon Peter sobbed. You know the kind of emotional response where the tears flow from deep inside your being. Tears ran down his face, out of his eyes and nose. Deep sobs. Gut-wrenching groans. Uncontrollable tears. Everything seemed over. Nothing had meaning. He never ever imagined that he would fail in this way. Not only had he failed his friend at this time of greatest need, but he had failed in front of the entire world. What humiliation . . . embarrassment . . . shame . . . and despair!

Unlike Judas, another disciple who had failed, Simon Peter decided to move on from this moment. Judas felt there was no hope for his life after he betrayed Jesus for thirty pieces of silver. Judas believed he could never be forgiven, that he was beyond redemption; so he took his own life. Somehow, Peter pushed beyond his despair and kept moving forward.

4. *Fear and disillusionment stole Peter's confidence and reduced his vision for the future.*

Simon Peter didn't take his own life like Judas did. But the gospel of John records Peter's struggle with shame and despair:

- He hid in fear—afraid that the Jewish religious leaders would kill him too (John 20:19).
- He decided to leave "ministry" and return to his known trade of fishing (John 21:3).
- His confidence was shaken. When the resurrected Jesus asked him, "Simon, do you love me?" Peter could hardly muster an answer, "Yes, Lord, you know that I love you" (John 21:16).

Coming face-to-face with our own selfishness and sinfulness is life-altering, but it's a necessary step to be used by God. Can you imagine the great loss to the church if Simon Peter had remained lost in despair? Thankfully he moved on, and Jesus forgave him. If you read John 21, you find amazing grace and acceptance as Christ gave Peter a second chance. Jesus assured the disciple that his life still counted; that there was a purpose for his life and God still wanted to use him. However, it wasn't until the Day of Pentecost that Simon Peter truly stepped into his new day.

5. *When Peter was baptized in the Holy Spirit—his life radically changed.*
Acts 2 provides the record of Simon Peter's transformation. He was in the upper room praying with the 120 when God poured out the Holy Spirit upon them all. Along with the others in the room, Peter heard the sound of a rushing wind and saw the huge flame of fire that came into the room and broke into 120 smaller flames that came to rest above the head of each person.

God's Spirit so impacted these people that they all began to speak out in prayer. Peter was right there in the middle of it all as the Holy Spirit filled them to overflowing. The noise was so loud and the commotion so great that the people gathered in the streets outside the house were bewildered about what was going on.

About that time, "Peter stood up . . . and addressed the crowd" (Acts 2:14). Simon Peter, the disciple who had denied Jesus just a few weeks before, took the lead! This was the same guy who could hardly speak when Jesus asked, "Do you love me?" The same guy who had been hiding in a room, terrified that the religious leaders would arrest him.

There he was standing boldly in front of several thousand people declaring to them that Jesus was alive. Remember, this was the same city where Jesus had been crucified. Peter was speaking just a mile or two from the place where the crucifixion had occurred. He was preaching to some of the same people who had yelled, "Crucify Him," when Jesus was on trial before Pilate. Simon Peter was risking his life by taking a stand at that moment.

But because he had been baptized in the Holy Spirit, he had the strength and courage to do what had not been possible for him to do before.

6. *Not only was Peter restored from his past—he was filled with God's overcoming power.*

It could have been the end for Simon Peter: the moment we read about in Luke 22:62. The moment he wept bitterly after the denials could have been the final word regarding his life. If he had remained overwhelmed by his shame, we would never have read another word about his life. He wouldn't have been one of the pillars of the early church. He would have stayed stuck in the shame of his past.

But Simon Peter didn't allow his failure to become final!

When Jesus rose, He made it His mission to forgive Simon Peter. Jesus pursued Peter and made sure the disciple knew that the past was in the past, and that the past didn't limit the potential or purpose of his future. Peter was forgiven. Peter was restored. He didn't have to live in shame. He had a future; he had hope.

But even that wasn't enough!

God couldn't have used Simon Peter like He did in Jerusalem (in Acts 2) if Peter hadn't been baptized in the Holy Spirit. Forgiveness was critical to Peter, but it wasn't enough. He needed restoration, but that wasn't enough. Simon Peter needed more. He needed to be infused with and empowered by the Holy Spirit.

7. God released supernatural power through Peter's life.
Supernatural things started to happen for Peter and through him.

The book of Acts records how the Holy Spirit impacts the life of someone like Simon Peter. In fact, the official title of the book is The Acts of the Apostles, which we might rephrase as The Acts of the Holy Spirit—Through the Lives of the Apostles. Peter was baptized in the Holy Spirit, and this marked the beginning of the supernatural in his ministry.

- He preached with great power, and 3,000 people were saved in one day (Acts 2).
- He prayed for a crippled man who was healed (Acts 3).
- He spoke boldly while on trial in front of the Sanhedrin, the same court that had so terrified him before (Acts 3–4).
- Mighty miracles happened as crowds brought their sick to him for prayer (Acts 5).
- He prayed for a crippled man who began to walk (Acts 9).
- He prayed for a dead woman and she came back to life (Acts 9).
- He received a vision during prayer that changed the way the church leaders thought about the Gentiles who needed the gospel (Acts 10).
- God sent an angel to break him out of prison (he was there for preaching about the resurrected Jesus) (Acts 12).

Remember, this was the same guy who denied Jesus and cowered in fear. On his own, he was inconsistent and ineffective. He was full of pride and self-consumed, but Jesus changed all that. Jesus forgave him and restored him. And when the Holy Spirit came upon Peter, he was transformed into a man who was bold, powerful, consistent, and filled with joy.

We simply can't overestimate the value of Simon Peter's experience with the Holy Spirit. He was never the same after he was baptized in the Holy Spirit. What he had before Acts 2 wasn't enough! He needed more. He needed to be empowered by the Holy Spirit. God took him from ordinary and inconsistent, and transformed him into someone who stepped into supernatural miracles that affected the entire world.

This is the will of God for your life!

What you have today is not enough, but the power of the Holy Spirit is enough! God has called you to so much more. His plan for you is to do so much more than just survive another week. He wants to use you to do the supernatural. Yes, you! He wants the Holy Spirit to be manifest in and released through your life. What you have been doesn't have to determine what you will be. Your past doesn't define your potential.

But what you are in yourself just isn't enough. You need more. You need to be baptized in the Holy Spirit. He provides the power you need for your life, and that power is more than enough!

DISCUSSION QUESTIONS FOR CHAPTER ONE

1. Describe a time in your life when you knew that what you had just wasn't enough.

2. Can you imagine what the disciples felt when Jesus unexpectedly ascended into heaven and left them here without Him? What words would you use to describe that emotion?

3. When you see someone who turns their life around, how is that motivating to you? In what ways does that give you hope?

4. When you consider the life of Simon Peter, what role did the Holy Spirit play in the radical transformation of his life?

5. In what area of your life do you most need the help of the Holy Spirit?

CHAPTER TWO
IT'S VISIBLE!

I want to live so that I am truly submitted to the Spirit's leading on a daily basis. Christ said it's better for us that the Spirit came and I want to live like that is true. I don't want to keep crawling when I have the ability to fly.[2]
—FRANCIS CHAN

Some things only change under the influence of the Holy Spirit.

The first defining moment happened in the back of an ambulance for Brian Bolt. The year was 2002, Brian was twenty-three years old, and his life had been in a self-destructive free fall. Arrested for drug use at the age of sixteen, Brian was given the opportunity to serve out his sentence by enlisting in the Navy rather than spend his days in the prison system.

The Navy was good for Brian. He got his GED, received training in his area of gifting, and obtained the needed discipline and structure necessary for a life free from drug use. However, the inner drive to use and abuse drugs never went away and before long Brian was back at it again while in port in San Diego, California. Friends invited Brian to cross the border into Mexico, where he found the opportunity to dive headlong into not only drug use but an entire drug industry.

Not only did Brian go AWOL, he used his Navy ID to serve as a drug mule and carried drugs across the border for compensation, both in money and in all the drugs he could ever hope to consume. For several years Brian was in and out of the brig, and in and out of serious trouble in so many ways. His life was spiraling out of control, and he was taking increasingly dangerous risks.

One day, back in his hometown of Cumberland, Maryland, Brian ended up in a bad situation. "I got caught trying to rob a guy," he reports, "and when the guy found out, he took a swing at me. I swung back, and knocked him to the ground. The second guy came at me, and as I was in the process of fighting him off, the first man got up off of the floor and pulled a gun. He pointed it at my head, and fired."

> When they prayed for me, I felt a surge of peace and power rush through my entire being.

Blood filled the barroom floor. The bullet pin-balled inside of Brian's skull and landed in his carotid artery, which slowed the bleeding enough for him to survive. Brian recounts that moment: "As I lay there on the floor realizing what had happened to me, I remember feeling relieved. There was nothing in life worth living for. I was so empty. I think I wanted to die."

Paramedics came and wheeled him into an ambulance. As the vehicle rushed toward the hospital, the EMT turned to Brian and said, "Son, you're probably going to die. Do you know Jesus as your Savior?" "No," Brian replied. The paramedic asked softly, "Would you like to pray with me right now to give your life to Christ?"

Brian said, "At that moment, something tugged at my heart and I knew that was what I needed in my life." So there, in the back of that ambulance, Brian prayed and invited Jesus to take over his life.

For seventy-five days, Brian was in and out of a medically induced coma. Doctors performed multiple surgeries not only to save his life but to recreate the entire left side of his face. Only the grace of God and the skillful hands of the surgeons saved Brian's life. When he was released from the hospital, he knew something had happened to him when he prayed to receive Christ, but he had no idea what to do with his newfound faith. So he went back to the streets and started hanging out with the same old group.

But God had a plan for Brian Bolt. One day while he was hanging out on the streets of San Diego, a group of guys from a Victory Outreach Men's Home approached him. "God has a plan for your life," they told Brian. "We have a place for you. If you come with us, we will help you learn what it is to live for God and to live for His purpose." So Brian agreed to go with them. He entered the Men's Home, a free recovery home provided by Victory Outreach Church with the goal of helping men and women get free from drugs and disciple them as followers of Christ.

One of the conditions of living in the Home was participation in Bible studies and prayer meetings several times a day. Participants learned the basics of following Christ. Brian started reading the Bible. He learned about prayer. And one day, during a prayer session, some of the guys laid their hands on Brian and he was baptized in the Holy Spirit.

Just like the Bible describes this experience in Acts 2:1–4, Brian was filled with the Holy Spirit and began to pray in a spiritual language. (We'll talk about this in a later chapter.) "When they prayed for me, I felt a surge of peace and power rush through my entire being. The emotional intensity of this moment was greater than any high I had ever experienced on drugs. Whatever this was, I wanted as much of it as I possibly could get!"

IT'S A CONTAGIOUS FREEDOM

Now let me tell you the rest of Brian's story. Shortly after being baptized in the Holy Spirit, he felt called to be a pastor. So he enrolled in the necessary training toward that end. In 2005, he joined the staff at Allison Park Church with the express intent of planting a church in the city of Pittsburgh that would be targeted for drug addicts, the broken, the formerly incarcerated, and those in need of hope.

Not only did Brian effectively plant City Reach Church Pittsburgh, he has also led the way in helping to establish over seventy City Reach churches all over the northeastern United States (with even more planned for the future). Many of these churches begin with the establishment of a Hope Home, a free recovery home for people who have tried everything and have no place else to go. These homes are giving hundreds of addicts a chance for a new life and a fresh start.

So what role does the baptism in the Holy Spirit play in helping people break free of addiction? What role did it play in Brian Bolt's life? What role does it play in the function of the Hope Homes, where so many are being set free?

> When you are filled with the Holy Spirit, His mighty power influences your thoughts, actions, and feelings.

"The baptism in the Holy Spirit is the key experience for an addict," Brian says. "Prior to that, you are fighting those old cravings out of your own effort and determination. But when the Holy Spirit fills you, you have a source of peace that overpowers everything else. Once I was baptized in the Holy Spirit, I felt a level of satisfaction in my soul that almost totally eliminated the magnetism of the old addictive cravings."

When describing the strategy of City Reach, Brian explains, "Not only do we want to bring people to a saving understanding of Jesus in their lives, we want to get them baptized in the Holy Spirit as soon as possible. As soon as a Hope Home resident is baptized in the Holy Spirit, everything about managing and leading them becomes so much easier. They have Someone inside of them giving them the power to overcome."

This powerful approach to freedom is described in the Bible. Look at what the apostle Paul wrote in his letter to the Ephesians:

> Be very careful, then, how you live—not as unwise
> but as wise, making the most of every opportunity,

because the days are evil. Therefore do not be foolish, but understand what the Lord's will is. Do not get drunk on wine, which leads to debauchery. Instead, be filled with the Spirit, speaking to one another with psalms, hymns, and songs from the Spirit. Sing and make music from your heart to the Lord, always giving thanks to God the Father for everything, in the name of our Lord Jesus Christ. (Ephesians 5:15–20)

Notice how these verses relate to our lives today:

- We live in evil days with temptations and trouble lurking all around us, which calls for us to live carefully and with great wisdom.
- It's foolish to allow ourselves to come under the influence of alcohol to the point of drunkenness because it leads us toward debauchery, which means the kind of self-destructive behavior that results from life being out of control; a life that makes us feel debased, ashamed, filled with regret.
- It isn't God's will that we experience that kind of pain. He has a better plan for us than a life filled with regret.
- It is God's will that we *be filled with the Spirit*, which leads to a life filled with peace, joy, and a life free of regret.

Compare the effects of alcohol and the impact of the Holy Spirit: both have an influential effect on us. When you drink, that substance affects your thoughts, your feelings, and your actions. When you are filled with the Holy Spirit, His mighty power influences your thoughts, actions, and feelings. For example, drinking alcohol to excess impairs judgment and causes behavior that is potentially destructive. Being filled with the Holy Spirit improves judgment and inspires life-giving behavior.

We need to be filled with the Holy Spirit! This experience is something more than what happens to us when we accept Jesus as our Savior. At that moment, we receive the Holy Spirit within our lives. In fact, we can't be saved apart from the regenerating work of the Holy Spirit. "But because of his great love for us, God, who is rich in mercy, made us alive with Christ even when we were dead in transgressions—it is by grace you have been saved"(Ephesians 2:4-5).

For those who believe in Jesus, that initial moment of Holy Spirit infusion is not the end of His work in our lives; it's just the beginning. The phrase in Ephesians 5:18 "be filled with the Spirit," actually reads like this in the original Greek: "Be being [constantly and continually] filled with the Holy Spirit." If we pursue the will of God, we will seek to bring our lives under the constant and continuous infilling of the Holy Spirit. This implies that we must cultivate a relationship with the Holy Spirit.

When we are baptized in the Holy Spirit, His infilling is an overpowering influence that improves our judgment and gives overflowing life to our souls. You see, some changes can only happen under the ongoing influence of the Holy Spirit. Some habits are just too hard to break in our own strength. Some tendencies are just too powerful to overcome. Some hurts are just too deep to process. Some pain is just too intense to move beyond.

But when the Holy Spirit fills our lives, habits break. Temptations are overcome. Hurts are healed. Pain no longer dominates. It's like a jet engine that propels an airplane to break the pull of gravity, lifting the heavy weight of that plane into the sky, thousands of feet into the air. It would be impossible for that airplane to break free of gravity without the engine. In a similar way, we need the power of the Holy Spirit to help us break free of the "gravity" of sin and despair and destructive habits.

IT'S A VISIBLE CHANGE

Let me tell you how the Holy Spirit totally changed my grandfather's life. Thomas Leake worked in the coal mines as a boy because his father was an alcoholic and couldn't support the family. Thomas brought his paycheck home every week and handed it over to his mother so the family would have money for food. Because he was working, he had to quit school at an early age, which created a deep-seated anger and frustration that he had hit a dead end so early in life.

After he married my grandmother, they moved onto a piece of land, started a farm on the side, and began to raise a family. My dad (his son) recalls, "He was a hard man: angry all the time, always in a fight, a chain-smoker, depressed. He never went to church and had little use for the things of God."

Each day he went off to work. While eating his lunch in the cafeteria, he would drink coffee in a company mug. When he finished the coffee, he slipped the mug into his lunch bucket. He did this daily, stealing mugs until the family had a large collection at home. The family never knew the mugs were stolen.

One day, someone invited him to a revival meeting. When the speaker gave the altar call, my grandfather shocked the world when he walked to the front to surrender his life to Christ.

Shortly after his conversion, Thomas Leake was baptized in the Holy Spirit. This baptism had several effects on my grandfather's life. First of all, it gave him the power to quit smoking. Shortly after experiencing the outpouring of the Holy Spirit in his life, he felt prompted to throw every cigarette he owned and his tobacco and pipe into the coal-burning stove. He never touched tobacco again.

Second, he felt convicted about his petty thefts. One night, shortly after his Holy Spirit baptism, my grandmother looked in the cupboard and couldn't find a single mug. When she asked my grandfather about this, he confessed what he had done and told her he had taken everything he had ever stolen back to the company, confessed to his foreman, and made things right before God.

Third, the anger in his life disappeared. The frustration was gone. He stopped fighting. He even became a bit tender and was touched to the point of tears when hearing a story about the grace of God in someone's life. He not only raised his family to love God but he served as a lay preacher at several outreaches around the town. God took a man who was filled with anger and transformed him into a man who was filled with peace and under the influence of the Holy Spirit.

This transformation had a powerful impact on my dad. In fact, it was a significant factor in his deciding to go into the ministry. He saw the miraculous change happen in his own family and he wanted God to use him to help others experience that same kind of change. This is the result of being filled with the Holy Spirit.

> When we declare the value and worth of God and we recognize the person and power of Jesus, we join forces with the Holy Spirit.

IT ALL BEGINS WITH WORSHIP

The challenge of Ephesians 5:18 is to be continually and constantly filled with the Holy Spirit. That sounds great! We want God's will to be fulfilled in our lives. We don't want a life filled with debauchery and regret. We want a life that is filled with power and peace and life. So how in the world does that happen? Paul provides some advice:

> Be filled with the Spirit, speaking to one another with psalms, hymns, and songs from the Spirit. Sing and make music from your heart to the Lord, always giving thanks to God the Father for everything, in the name of our Lord Jesus Christ. (Ephesians 5:18–20)

"Be filled with the Spirit" is the command. Then the process recommended for this immediately follows: "speaking to one another with psalms, hymns, and songs from the Spirit" (spontaneous singing from the heart). Then Paul adds: "sing and make music from your heart to the Lord, always giving thanks to God the Father for everything."

Paul's words are filled with wisdom. First, the Holy Spirit is attracted to our choice to worship. When we declare the value and worth of God and we recognize the person and power of Jesus, we join forces with the Holy Spirit. You see, the Holy Spirit's primary work in the world is to bring glory and honor to Jesus. So anytime we choose to honor Jesus, we magnetize our hearts to the Holy Spirit.

Second, the Holy Spirit draws close to us as we choose to worship. Remember that the Holy Spirit is the third person of the Trinity. He is every bit as much God as is the Father and Jesus. When we worship, He draws near to us in a real and tangible way. "You are holy, enthroned on the praises of [your people]" (Psalm 22:3). As we worship, it's as though He steps into the room and rests upon our hearts as His throne.

Third, the Holy Spirit is released within and around us as we worship. The verses in Ephesians tell us that we are to sing songs out of our spirit and to make music in our hearts. Notice the emphasis is on our hearts. We are spiritual beings. The center of our body is the place where our spirit resides. So we sing or praise out of the depths of our being.

Jesus promised this in John 7:37–39, "On the last and greatest day of the festival, Jesus stood and said in a loud voice, 'Let anyone who is thirsty come to me and drink. Whoever believes in me, as Scripture has said, rivers of living water will flow from within them.' By this He meant the Spirit, whom those who believed in Him were later to receive." "Rivers of living water will flow *from within* them." As we worship, we release the river of living water that resides within us. As we vocalize our praise, an explosion of life is released from the center of our person. We feel the rush of God's presence being released out of our hearts, through our lips, and overflowing our lives. It's powerful!

Notice that the recommended actions of Ephesians 5:18–20 are vocal: sing, make music, speak to one another, give thanks. The process of being filled with the Spirit requires that we speak, sing, and declare things out of our lips. When we vocalize our praise, we release something out of our spirits. The Holy Spirit is released out of our inner being, like a flood or a raging river, as we speak forth our praise to God.

Why don't we start there right now? Before we go any further with this discussion about the baptism in the Holy Spirit, let's begin by vocalizing our worship. Find a quiet place where you feel comfortable praying out loud and confess this prayer to God.

> *God, I thank You for who You are in my life. You are the Creator of the universe. You are the Sustainer of my life. In You, I find everything that I need.*
>
> *Jesus, I thank You for dying on the cross for me. Thank You for shedding Your blood to pay for my sin. Thank You for Your resurrection. I declare that You are alive and that You are doing an amazing work in the world and in my life.*
>
> *Holy Spirit, I invite You to take over my life. Thank You for helping me worship. I open my heart to You. Have Your way in my life. Fill me. Overflow me. Release the raging river of life within my soul. In Jesus' name, amen.*

DISCUSSION QUESTIONS FOR CHAPTER TWO

1. When you look back on your life, who has been the greatest positive influence for you? What made that person so influential?

2. Read Ephesians 5:15–20. There are times that drugs, alcohol, and even certain relationships can have an unhealthy influence on us. What are some negative effects of unhealthy influences?

3. How is the Holy Spirit the best influence you could ever experience?

4. Read John 7:37–39. What do you picture when you hear Jesus' description?

5. The verses in Ephesians 5 teach us that the Holy Spirit is activated when we start to worship. If you are going through a challenging time in your life, one choice is to worship. If you don't worship, what other choices could you make?

6. What one thing will you do, after this, to activate the Holy Spirit in your life?

CHAPTER THREE

IT'S SUPERNATURAL!

Jesus gives us the gift of the Holy Spirit, yet when the Spirit comes, He is loaded with packages! He desires to release much more in us and through us than we could ever imagine. These gifts are given for delivery, not for accumulation. We receive them to pass them on to others.[3]

—JACK HAYFORD

For Johannes Amritzer, childhood wasn't easy by any stretch of the imagination. His father was a criminal, in and out of prison. His mother often moved from one abusive boyfriend to the next looking for a place to find refuge. Due to this dysfunctional home life, Johannes bounced from foster home to foster home or by necessity lived for months with grandma, aunts, and uncles.

Johannes grew up fighting for his life. He turned to alcohol, sex, and crime to cope and survive. But deep in his spirit he sensed that he was built for something more. He describes one quiet moment when he was on a platform getting ready to catch a train in Germany.

Early one morning, he stood overlooking the train station and all he could see were drug addicts, homeless people, and the prostitutes who were waking up to a new day of misery. At that moment he heard a Voice say to him, "One day, I will use you to reach people just like this." Johannes admits, "Now I know that Voice was the Holy Spirit. But at the time, I had no idea what was happening to me. I thought it might be God talking to me, but I assumed I wasn't worthy of a visitation like that."

Eventually, Johannes' older brother became a Christian. Because of his salvation experience, he did his best to convince his younger brother to give his life to Jesus as well. "It was a joke to me," Johannes recounts. "I thought he had lost his mind, and I consistently let him know about it." After refusing to attend church many times, one Sunday Johannes finally showed up.

During that service, his first time to be in church in a long time, Johannes sensed the same presence he had experienced on the train platform in Germany. By the end of the evening, Johannes had prayed to give his life to Christ.

Shortly after this moment of decision, a youth leader explained to him about the baptism in the Holy Spirit. The leader shared that being baptized in the Holy Spirit would enable God to use Johannes in a supernatural way. So they prayed. Right there, Johannes experienced the outpouring of the Holy Spirit in his life. Out of his lips came the release of power and praise, and he was changed.

No one could have predicted the degree to which Johannes would be used by God. Within a year he was preaching on the streets and winning to Jesus hundreds of skinheads, drug addicts, and other troubled youth in the regions of Sweden, Poland, Germany, and the Czech Republic through Teen Challenge, a youth rehab ministry. The gift of evangelism was obvious in his life, and the Holy Spirit was using him to prove that Jesus is alive and active in the world to rescue us from sin.

As Johannes ministered, supernatural things began to occur. Sick people were healed. Those tormented by demon spirits were set free. The crowds he ministered to continued to grow as word spread about the young evangelist God was using in supernatural ways.

My friendship with Johannes began in 2002. He and I met when he spoke at a conference I attended in Hampton, Virginia. I sat mesmerized as I listened to him recount how God was doing extraordinary miracles through his ministry overseas. After preaching in Sweden and around Europe, God had called Johannes to focus his energies on sharing the message of a risen Jesus with people groups that had never heard of Jesus. Mission S.O.S. was born out of this calling.

One of my favorite miracle stories took place at one of his festivals in Bulgaria. A crippled Muslim woman was attending the festival. For the first time, she heard how Jesus, who is God in the flesh, had come to earth on a mission to save us. She heard how He died on the cross for her sin and how He rose from the dead. She heard how He was healing people, right there in Bulgaria.

Johannes explained, "She had been crippled for so long, that all the muscles in her legs had atrophied. They hung from her body like spaghetti strands, limp, skinny, damaged legs. Her Muslim friends lifted her out of her wheelchair and literally threw her up on stage, demanding: "Heal her in Jesus' name if you can!"

"I saw in her eyes the faith to be healed," Johannes continued. "And all of a sudden, I felt a rush of faith within me. The Holy Spirit was shouting to my mind that He was going to heal her body. So before I knew it, I had picked her up, holding her under her arms. I heard myself say, 'I will not let you down until you walk!'"

"As soon as I said it," Johannes confessed, "I thought to myself, *that's crazy! What are you saying? Now you're really on the spot! What if nothing happens? How long can you hold this woman up in front of this enormous crowd of people?* But I felt the prompting to say it again, so I repeated, 'I will not let you go until you walk.' Then all of a sudden the woman put her feet on the ground and began to take steps. Her legs were so weak she couldn't walk without wobbling and without support. But as she stepped out in faith, her legs grew stronger. Right before the eyes of this Islamic crowd, Jesus showed Himself to be alive by healing this woman's broken body."

Over the years of our friendship, I have heard Johannes tell hundreds of such stories. After a few years, I decided to go with him on one of these trips to see some of this for myself. I wasn't disappointed. Deaf people began to hear. Blind eyes were opened. Demon-possessed people cried out as they were set free. It was just like the moments I had read about in the Bible, but now I was living them firsthand. With every trip, I grew more and more hungry to see God's power released in my own life.

"How is this possible?" I asked Johannes early in our friendship. He replied, "For me, the journey into the supernatural began when I was baptized in the Holy Spirit. None of this would be possible in my life without that first experience." That's what so amazing about God's plan for His people. The baptism

The baptism in the Holy Spirit is for *every* believer.

in the Holy Spirit isn't just for the super-Christian who travels the world and speaks to thousands in a festival. The baptism in the Holy Spirit is for *every* believer.

Listen to what Simon Peter said just after his experience with the baptism in the Holy Spirit, "Repent and be baptized, *every one of you*, in the name of Jesus Christ for the forgiveness of your sins. And you will receive the gift of the Holy Spirit. The promise is for you and for your children and for all who are far off—for all whom the Lord our God will call" (Acts 2:38–39 ESV, emphasis added). This promise is for *you*! It's for your children!

WHAT DOES IT MEAN TO BE BAPTIZED IN THE HOLY SPIRIT?

Jesus challenged His disciples and made them a promise. "Do not leave Jerusalem, but wait for the gift my Father promised. For John baptized with water, but in a few days you will be baptized with the Holy Spirit" (Acts 1:4–5). He was warning them, "Don't try to accomplish the mission without the power. Wait . . . receive . . . then take this message into every part of the earth." Then He made the promise: *"You will be baptized with the Holy Spirit."*

To understand this statement we need to see the comparison. When Jesus referred to John, He was talking about the man known as John the Baptist. John came prior to Jesus. He announced to the people of his day that the kingdom of God was coming to the earth. He challenged his hearers to repent (turn from) their sinful selfish ways and surrender to God. Those who heeded his teachings submitted to a symbolic initiation rite called baptism. They were immersed in water, often in the Jordan River.

By being baptized in this way, these people declared that they were leaving their former way of life to follow after God. They went down into the waters as sinful persons, and came up out of the water, washed, clean, and new. Baptism was all about beginning something new. It was about being dipped under and enveloped by the waters of the river.

The word *baptize* means "to dip under the water." We use a similar word in the English language. The word *capsize* means for a boat to turn over and sink in the water. Every water baptism we see in the Bible involves a person being submerged in a body of water and coming back up completely wet. Jesus was saying to the disciples, "In a few days, you'll be dipped under, totally submerged in, and completely enveloped by the Holy Spirit. And when that happens to you, you'll be filled with the power necessary to prove and witness to My resurrection."

Think about it! Dipped under and enveloped, not by a substance like water, but in a relationship with the Holy Spirit. We haven't talked much about exactly who the Holy Spirit is up until this moment, but we need to do so now. The Holy Spirit is the third person of the Godhead. God is three persons in one being: the Father, the Son, and the Holy Spirit. Just prior to His crucifixion, Jesus introduced the Holy Spirit to the disciples.

WHO IS THE HOLY SPIRIT?

Just before Jesus died, He encouraged His disciples with this, "And I will ask the Father, and he will give you another Helper, to be with you forever, even the Spirit of truth, whom the world cannot receive, because it neither sees him nor knows him. You know him, for he dwells with you and will be in you" (John 14:16-17 ESV).

1. *The Holy Spirit is just like Jesus.*

Jesus said the Father "will give you another Helper." The word *another* in the Greek implies, "someone who is just like me—who is taking my place." Can you imagine if you could do life with Jesus walking beside you physically, at every moment? You could consult Him about issues at home or at work.

> The Holy Spirit strengthens me. He infuses His thoughts into me.

You could ask Him to teach you what to do in a confusing relationship. He would be there to help you when you had a need or didn't know how to pray.

Having the Holy Spirit with you gives you the same benefit. He is the same in essence as Jesus. He is a part of the Godhead just like Jesus. He knows everything God knows, because He is part of the Godhead. You might not be able to see Him, but He is as present with you as anyone ever could be and more. He can advise you, equip you, comfort you, and empower you for life.

2. *The Holy Spirit adds life into me.*

Jesus called the Holy Spirit the "Helper," which in the Greek is *paraclete*. The best way to define this word is by contrast. You understand the word *parasite*. It's a living entity that attaches itself to you to suck the life from you. That's not even fun to think about. Once when I traveled out of the country on a mission trip I came back with a parasite in my stomach. I was super sick and weak. I felt like the parasite was literally draining the life out of me!

In contrast, we can define a *paraclete* as a living entity that attaches Himself to me to add life into me. The Holy Spirit strengthens me. He infuses His thoughts into me. He releases to me His emotions: joy, peace, love, patience. He shares His power with me. He gives me what I need at the moment I need it.

3. *The Holy Spirit walks with me through life.*
Jesus said the Holy Spirit, "the Spirit of truth," will "be with you forever." The Holy Spirit teaches and instructs and reminds us of who Jesus is and what the Bible says. He reinforces us in every way.

* * *

Every person who believes in Jesus receives such companionship from the Holy Spirit. He begins to dwell within your life at the moment you confess Christ as your Lord and Savior. In fact, the Holy Spirit is like the "welcoming committee" into God's family. As soon as you pray to receive Christ, the Holy Spirit ignites life on the inside of you. He takes your dead soul and makes it alive. The instant He does that you know it. Romans 8:16 says, "The Spirit himself testifies with our spirit that we are God's children."

So hear this now. The moment you are saved, you receive the Holy Spirit. He lives in you from the moment you become a Christian. And since He lives within you, He immediately begins to give you the capacity to be a better person than you were before. He releases all that He is to you. This moment happened for the original disciples just after Jesus' resurrection. John 20 records the moment when Jesus appeared to the disciples in His resurrected body. "Peace be with you! As the Father has sent me, I am sending you." And with that He breathed on them and said, "Receive the Holy Spirit" (John 20:21–22).

At that moment, Jesus imparted to them the Holy Spirit, just like it happens for us when we pray for salvation. The Holy Spirit took up residence in the disciples' hearts. They received the Holy Spirit as Jesus breathed the Spirit into them.

You might think that would have been enough!

But just a few days later, Jesus told these same disciples, "Do not leave Jerusalem, but wait for the gift my Father promised. . . . For John baptized with water, but in a few days you will be baptized with the Holy Spirit" (Acts 1:4–5).

The disciples had received the Holy Spirit in John 20. But they had not yet been baptized in the Holy Spirit. Jesus was promising to "dip them under" the Holy Spirit. There is a difference between these two experiences. Having received the Holy Spirit at salvation is the main thing, but if we are to function in the supernatural, we need something more.

WHAT DOES IT MEAN TO BE CLOTHED IN POWER?

This is where it helps to consider different gospel histories. We can hear the words of Jesus from several observers; each account adding value to the overall picture. Luke wrote of the post-resurrection moments that Jesus spent with His disciples. (Remember that Luke penned both the book of Luke and the book of Acts). Here's what Jesus said:

> "I am going to send you what my Father has promised; but stay in the city until you have been *clothed with power* from on high." (Luke 24:49, emphasis added)

The word *clothed* means "to sink into or be plunged into one's clothing; to be arrayed in a garment; to be endued with or placed within." The word *power* is the same word that we saw used in Acts 1. It's the Greek word *dunamis,* which is the root of our English word *dynamite.*

Jesus promised to give His disciples some "power clothes" to wear. They were to walk around clothed in and surrounded by the explosive, life-giving power of the Holy Spirit. Everywhere they went and everything they touched would be impacted by these "power clothes." This experience was something more than what happened to the disciples in John 20. They had already received the Holy Spirit when Jesus promised to give them even more. He breathed on them, and then He wanted to clothe them with power.

CAN I REALLY BE "ON FIRE"?

Let's look at another Bible passage. The apostle John recorded the words of John the Baptist when he introduced Jesus to the world:

> "I baptize you with water. But one who is more powerful than I will come [Jesus], the straps of whose sandals I am not worthy to untie [He is so much greater than I am that I am not worthy even to untie His sandals.] He will baptize you with the Holy Spirit and *fire*." (Luke 3:16, emphasis added).

So let's put it all together:

- The disciples had already received the Holy Spirit (just like we do when we are saved).
- Jesus promised them something more.
- He promised to dip them under or into the Holy Spirit so they would be completed covered by and immersed in His presence.
- When they came out of that baptism experience, they would be clothed with power.
- It would be as though they had been baptized in the fire of God.

I love how Johannes puts it, "When you are baptized in the Holy Spirit, God dresses you in the 'fire clothes' of Jesus." In other words, you walk around wearing the fiery power of God on your life. And just as Jesus did the supernatural through the power of the Holy Spirit, so you can expect to see the supernatural through that same Holy Spirit power. It's as though Jesus went to heaven and left behind His fire clothes for every believer to wear.

There's a great story in 2 Kings about the powerful old prophet Elijah and his spiritual son, Elisha. God used Elijah to do amazing miracles. This prophet experienced incredible answers to his prayers. Once, God answered his prayer and raised a boy back to life who had died. When God took Elijah to heaven, the prophet left behind his mantle or outer cloak for the younger man Elisha to wear. The cloak was filled with the sweat and aroma of Elijah.

> [Elisha] took the cloak that had fallen from Elijah and struck the water [of the Jordan River] with it. "Where now is the LORD, the God of Elijah?" he asked. When he struck the water, it divided to the right and to the left and he crossed over. The company of the prophets [bystanders] from Jericho, who were watching, said, "The spirit of Elijah is resting on Elisha." (2 Kings 2:14–15)

Can you see the parallels here? As Elijah left his mantle for Elisha, so Jesus left behind His "mantle" for us. He wants us to carry the same Spirit upon us that was upon Him. He wants to clothe us in power. He wants to baptize us in the Holy Spirit and in fire. He wants us to put on His fire clothes and walk around as instruments of Holy Spirit explosiveness.

Do you long for this?

Do you want the Father to clothe you in power?

Do you want to wear the fire clothes of Jesus?

As we are baptized in the Holy Spirit, we can enter the challenging places of life and say, "Where now is the power of Jesus?" And as we step out in faith to be used by God, He will release miracles through us to the world.

One of the great moments for me as a father happened a few years ago. My oldest son, David, felt a call into the ministry. He gave his life to Christ at a young age, and when he was a teen, he was baptized in the Holy Spirit. When he graduated from high school, he went on a mission trip to Tanzania where he prayed for the sick during the meetings.

I'll never forget his report of that trip. "Dad, I prayed for a man who was blind. His eyes were all cloudy. And as I prayed in the name of Jesus, I could see the cloudiness disappear. He started waving his arms, and we both knew what had happened: He could see!" Then David added, "It was totally awesome!"

Once you have had an experience like that, you will never view the Christian life in the same way. No longer is it a philosophy of life or a set of moral teachings. No longer is being a Christian just about going to church and trying to be a good person. When you are baptized in the Holy Spirit and you step out to see the power of God released through your life, the Christian life becomes an adventure of following a risen Jesus and showing the world that He is alive and still doing miracles in the world today.

DISCUSSION QUESTIONS FOR CHAPTER THREE

1. Have you ever worn special equipment or a uniform for a job or a sport? If so, why was it necessary to be clothed like that?
2. Read Luke 24:49. How would you explain this promise to someone?
3. If we really believed we were "clothed" in the power of God, how would we act and react in life?
4. Read 2 Kings 2:14. Elisha picked up the miraculous cloak or mantle of Elijah and then acted in faith. What would it mean for you to take hold of the "mantle" or fire clothes of Jesus by the power of the Holy Spirit?

CHAPTER FOUR

IT'S VERBAL!

*If it is in the Bible, it is so. It's not even to be prayed about.
It's to be received and acted upon. Inactivity is a robber which steals
blessings. Increase comes by action, by using what we have and know. Your
life must be one of going on from faith to faith.*[4]
—SMITH WIGGLESWORTH

To be honest, I had some bad experiences as the son of a Pentecostal minister!

I was baptized in the Holy Spirit on October 20, 1980. I'll never forget it, but not just because it was an experience that changed my life. I'll never forget it because it was the culmination of a five-month season where I questioned everything about this experience in general.

Just a few months prior, I had attended a youth camp. One evening the message was about the experience that Jesus called being baptized in the Holy Spirit. At the conclusion of the message, the speaker called us forward if we wanted to be filled with the Holy Spirit. Well, I was ready. I couldn't wait for the moment to arrive. The message had filled me with such vision and hunger for the presence and power of God that I ran to the front as soon as they gave us the opportunity.

I understood what the Bible taught about this moment. In just about every case in the book of Acts when people were baptized in the Holy Spirit, they responded to His presence by declaring their praise out loud.

- "All of them were filled with the Holy Spirit and began to speak in other tongues as the Spirit enabled them" (Acts 2:4).
- "The Holy Spirit came on all who heard the message. The [Jewish] believers who had come with Peter were astonished that the gift of the Holy Spirit had been poured out even on the Gentiles [non-Jews]. For they heard them speaking in tongues and praising God" (Acts 10:44–46).
- "When Paul placed his hands on them, the Holy Spirit came on them, and they spoke in tongues and prophesied" (Acts 19:6).

So when I went to the front to receive the baptism in the Holy Spirit, I fully expected to speak in tongues. The speaker that evening had done a great job of painting the picture of what happened to those who experienced the Holy Spirit in the book of Acts. So I was ready, and so were those who were praying for me.

I guess it shows that I was loved, but there were way too many people converged to pray for me that night. It was a hot summer evening, and about fifteen of my friends and youth leaders were gathered around me. Most of them placed a hand on my head, or shoulder, or arm. The Bible talks about laying hands on people in prayer, and these good friends were reaching out to encourage me. Some were swaying as they prayed, so this large crowd of people (with me in the center) began to sway back and forth like the waves of the ocean. Many of them were praying out loud; some were shouting encouragements.

"Receive! In Jesus name! Now speak it out! Release the gift! Be filled! Be filled!"

I sometimes joke that someone was saying, "Hold on, hold on!" and another was saying, "Let go, let go!" I'm not sure if that's true or not, but I can tell you that I was thoroughly confused, frustrated, and overwhelmed by the expectation for me to perform some spiritual feat on cue. It was religious pandemonium. And it went on and on for what seemed like hours (although it was probably only about fifteen minutes).

Finally, I got the courage to break out of the circle of expectation. I retreated to the front row and sat with my head in my hands, hoping people would just leave me alone to think for a minute. Some friends came over to sit next to me and kept praying. I had to ask them to stop, and explained that I just needed a few minutes to pray on my own. They respected that, but I could tell they were disappointed. They wanted me to experience a breakthrough in this area so badly, and nothing visible seemed to happen.

My reaction to that experience was to question everything. My thoughts went something like this:

- *Is something wrong with me? Do I have sin in my life and that's why I couldn't speak in tongues?*
- *Maybe everyone is just crazy? How can this be from God?*
- *What in the world is this "speaking in tongues" thing anyway? Is it really in the Bible? Is it necessary? Why do they make such a big deal out of it? It just seems weird to me!*
- *What does speaking in tongues have to do with the baptism in the Holy Spirit? Can't I just be filled with the Spirit without all this other stuff?*
- *I'm more of a private person, so can't I just experience this in my own way? Do I really have to declare anything out loud to be baptized in the Holy Spirit?*

For five months, I wrestled through these questions. I asked my dad to sit down with me and I interrogated him on what the Bible teaches. He calmly answered every one of my questions from the Bible. I had to admit that being filled with the Spirit was in there. There was no denying the verses listed in the book of Acts and in other books like 1 Corinthians. But I still wasn't ready to deal with the disappointment I felt from that night at youth camp. So I decided just to put the whole idea on the shelf for a while . . . but God wouldn't allow it. Every place I went people were talking about it.

I showed up at church, and the speaker selected as his text a passage of Scripture that dealt with the baptism in the Holy Spirit. A few days later, I attended a youth small group, and the students leading the meeting brought up the topic and shared their testimonies about being filled with the Spirit. Even when I turned on a Christian radio station, someone was preaching about it. Dare I say it was kind of spooky?

> The baptism in the Holy Spirit is a promise that is given to all who show up for it.

Finally, I had my moment of breakthrough. It was in my living room. It was after our youth small group had met and once again this was the topic of discussion. Out of frustration, I said to one of my friends, "I give up! I know God wants me to experience the baptism in the Holy Spirit, but I just don't think it will ever happen for me." My friend gently and quietly challenged me, "Let's pray right now."

As we prayed, just the two of us in a quiet room, I began to feel something happen within me. It was that warm sensation in my chest that I often felt when I was in church or in a season of worship. It grew stronger and stronger as I verbalized praise to God.

Then my friend said to me, "God is all over you! I can sense that He's baptizing you in the Holy Spirit at this moment. Now, what you need to do is tune into what He says to you. When you hear a syllable in your spirit that you don't recognize in English, just speak it out loud. That's what speaking in tongues is. It is speaking in a language that God supernaturally gives to you. So just say what you hear in your heart."

And just like that, I spoke out in a spiritual language. As I did, I felt that rush of the river of the Holy Spirit flowing from within me. It was amazing. So I kept on praying out loud what the Holy Spirit gave me to say. As I did this, His presence flooded my being over and over again. An hour in prayer this way felt like just a few minutes.

I have never been the same since that night!

I realize that you may have some of the same questions I wrestled through. So just like my father did, I want to calmly and biblically address these questions one at a time. My dad sat with me at the kitchen table. We both pulled out our Bibles, and he took me through passage after passage to address my objections. So let's sit together for a moment and do the same.

QUESTION 1:
IS SOMETHING WRONG WITH ME?
DO I HAVE SIN IN MY LIFE AND THAT'S WHY I CAN'T
SPEAK IN TONGUES?

What a deflating feeling to believe that God has singled you out as unworthy. That was the bottom line of how I felt: rejected, unworthy, exposed, and judged before the entire world and found wanting. No one should ever feel this way. So often, where this experience is concerned, well-meaning people put a huge amount of pressure on those seeking to be baptized in the Holy Spirit. The result is that when people fail to speak in tongues, they feel like something is wrong with them or wrong with the entire idea of Holy Spirit baptism.

First of all, we need to understand that the baptism in the Holy Spirit is a *gift*. This is how Jesus described the experience to the disciples. "Do not leave Jerusalem, but wait for the *gift* my Father promised" (Acts 1:4, emphasis added). The word used here in the Greek is *epaggelia*, which means: "to announce the fulfillment of a promised good thing to be given."

The baptism in the Holy Spirit is a promise that is given to all who show up for it. It isn't something we earn by being worthy. It's something we obtain simply by showing up to receive what God has promised to give us.

I'm writing this book, in a coffee shop, at the moment. Earlier today, I received an email notice from this shop announcing to me that if I showed up today I would receive a free specialty drink because last month I had a birthday. The coffee shop gave me an *epaggelia* (a declared promise of a good thing to be given). When I showed up to receive my free drink, I wasn't thinking about whether or not I was worthy to obtain this Grande Cappuccino. I didn't do any self-examination before I made the request to the barista. I just asked to receive what the shop had promised me.

In a similar way, the Father promises to give the Holy Spirit to anyone who asks. It's a gift that He gives by grace. None of us will ever deserve this gift, but God promises to give the Holy Spirit to all those who ask. In another place, Jesus said, "If you then, though you are evil, know how to give good gifts to your children, how much more will your Father in heaven give the Holy Spirit to those who ask him" (Luke 11:13)!

First, the baptism in the Holy Spirit is a *gift* that is promised by the Father; we cannot earn it. Second, the baptism in the Holy Spirit is a *grant* that is conveyed by God so that we can begin to operate according to His purpose.

When I went to college, I applied to several organizations to receive a grant: funds conveyed to me to pay for my studies. Several of these organizations approved me and released a grant to me so I could afford to do what I wouldn't have been able to do otherwise. This is what the Father wants for you and me. He wants to convey the Holy Spirit on us as a grant, giving us the capacity to be a witness for the resurrected Jesus, which we can't accomplish without His help.

You don't have to be worthy to receive this gift or to be given this grant. You just need to show up and ask for it. God doesn't reject you and He doesn't judge you as inferior or lacking. He doesn't single you out as someone who is a disappointment to Him. He doesn't expose you as a fraud or a failure. He wants to give you what He promised. I can say from personal experience that it's fruitless to spend a lot of time grieving over your own unworthiness.

Yes, if you look close enough at my life, you'll find plenty of reasons why God should just leave me and reject me. I fail. I'm a sinner. I fall short of perfection. My life is often selfish and sinful.

But God didn't save me because I was worthy. He saved me because He loved me. I don't understand it; but it's true. He loves me, and He isn't going to change His mind about that fact. Not only does He love me, He accepts me and wants to do amazing things in my life.

In the same way, the Father wants to give me the Holy Spirit in greater measure just because He has chosen to do that for me. I'm His child; He's my Father. He knows how to give His kids His best gifts. So if I ask for the outpouring of the Holy Spirit in my life, He has promised to give it to me. I don't have to earn it. I don't have to prove that I'm worthy of it. All I can do is receive it.

QUESTION 2:
IS EVERYONE JUST CRAZY?
CAN THIS REALLY BE FROM GOD?

This is often the response I hear to the very idea of speaking in tongues. It just sounds odd, doesn't it? Maybe it's just me, but the first time I heard of this, I thought, *What? Speaking in a language you have never studied? Impossible! Weird! Spooky!*

Then I heard a woman speaking in tongues in church. I think I was seven or eight years old. She was seated in the pew just behind me, praying in a very high-pitched tone, and it startled me. All of a sudden, she closed her eyes, started to cry, and belted out a prayer in a language that sounded something like Chinese to me. It freaked me out! I thought to myself, *I will do a lot of things in life, but I will never do that!*

Later, as I read the Bible for myself, I discovered this is something real. It's biblical. Over centuries, millions of people have practiced it. The apostle Paul said, "I thank God that I speak in tongues more than all of you" (1 Corinthians 14:18). He was writing to the Corinthian church, which was well known for their use and pursuit of spiritual gifts. Obviously, for Paul, this was a regular and normal experience.

Once I had prayed in tongues, I understood that this experience isn't spooky at all. I don't have to stop being the quiet, introverted, private person that I am to pray in a spiritual language. I never have prayed like that woman who scared me to death when I was seven. My nature isn't to be overly emotional, even when God is working in my life. I haven't had to become loud or emotional to experience the Holy Spirit's work in my life. The great thing is, people who are naturally loud and emotional don't have to be like me. They can be who they are and respond to God according to their own personality.

QUESTION 3:
WHAT IN THE WORLD IS SPEAKING
IN TONGUES ANYWAY?

"Speaking in tongues" is a way to describe "speaking in another language." In the book of Revelation, heaven is described as a place where every tribe and "tongue" will be present. "After these things I looked, and behold, a great multitude which no one could number, of all nations, tribes, peoples, and tongues, standing before the throne and before the Lamb . . . " (Revelation 7:9 NKJV). The word *tongue* is used to describe various language groups. What makes the biblical experience of speaking in tongues unique is that it's a supernatural act, a language miracle. We speak out in a language we have never studied and don't naturally understand.

The first time this occurred in history is recorded in Acts 2. The people who had gathered there heard others speaking "in tongues" and knew that a miracle was happening. "Now there were staying in Jerusalem God-fearing Jews from every nation. . . . When they heard this sound, a crowd came together in bewilderment, because each one heard their own language being spoken. Utterly amazed, they asked, 'Aren't all these who are speaking Galileans? Then how is it that each of us hears them in our native language'" (Acts 2:5–8)?

As we participate in this "language miracle," God does several things:

> What makes the biblical experience of speaking in tongues unique is that it's a supernatural act, a language miracle.

1. *He reveals Jesus to those who hear.* When the believers were first baptized in the Holy Spirit, the people around them said, "We hear them declaring the wonders of God in our own tongues! Amazed and perplexed, they asked one another, 'What does this mean?'"(Acts 2:11–12).

As you can imagine, this miracle of language was pretty convincing. The people knew such a thing could only happen if God were at work. Thousands gathered to hear Simon Peter speak because they had witnessed this language miracle. Speaking in tongues is just one of the many supernatural things that God wants to do in our lives.

My wife's grandparents (Lewie and Evelyn Spencer) were missionaries in Costa Rica back in the 1930s. They wanted to take the message of Jesus to tribes of people who had never heard about Him. Their only mode of transportation to these remote areas was on the back of a mule. So they traveled for days, over high mountains, to reach these tribes and share the good news of salvation.

On one occasion, they encountered a tribe that was completely unfamiliar to them. None of their interpreters knew the dialect. The Spencers tried to communicate, but nothing seemed to work, so they stopped and prayed. They gathered in a circle and prayed for God to help them. As they prayed, my wife's grandparents began to speak in tongues.

As soon as they started praying that way, the members of the tribe became animated. They began to jump up and down and wave their arms. It was obvious that something significant was happening. Within a few hours, they found an interpreter and he helped the Spencers communicate with the tribe. As soon as they started to converse, one of the tribe members asked, "How did you come to learn our language? When you gathered in that circle and started talking to the sky, one of you started telling us that God had sent you to us with some good news. How do you know our language?"

When they explained that God had performed a language-miracle through them and that He did this because He loved them, the entire tribe was ready to hear the message about Jesus Christ.

> The baptism in the Holy Spirit is the first step into a supernatural life.

2. He uses this to help us pray more effectively.

Most often, speaking in tongues is used privately and in prayer. The Holy Spirit prompts us to pray in a special prayer language. We don't know how to pray as well as the Holy Spirit does, so He helps us pray better.

Romans 8:26–27 says, "In the same way, the Spirit helps us in our weakness. We do not know what we ought to pray for, but the Spirit himself intercedes for us through wordless groans. And he who searches our hearts knows the mind of the Spirit, because the Spirit intercedes for God's people in accordance with the will of God."

First Corinthians 14:2 adds, "For anyone who speaks in a tongue *does not speak to people but to God.* Indeed, no one understands them; they utter mysteries by the Spirit" (emphasis added).

QUESTION 4:
IS SPEAKING IN TONGUES REALLY NECESSARY?

Many people ask, "Do I have to speak in tongues to be baptized in the Holy Spirit?" I like to respond with my father's explanation to me, "It's not that you *have* to speak in tongues; it's that you *get* to speak in tongues." You have the opportunity to allow the Holy Spirit to be released through you as you pray. The Spirit of God is praying through you as He is praying for you and for those in your world. That's amazing!

Every time people were baptized in the Holy Spirit in the book of Acts, they prayed aloud in a supernatural way. When the Holy Spirit comes upon you, He gives you power to prove that Jesus is alive. So the baptism in the Holy Spirit is the first step into a supernatural life. Not only does God want to do this language-miracle in you, He wants to use you to see many powerful and miraculous things happen in the name of Jesus.

Remember, the goal of the baptism in the Holy Spirit is not for you to speak in tongues. Did you hear that? That is *not* the goal. The goal of the baptism in the Holy Spirit is to give you power to prove that Jesus is alive. The baptism in the Holy Spirit is a gift that releases the power of God into and through your life. Speaking in another language is just the first miracle that God wants to do through you. It certainly isn't the last miracle He will do through you. He has so much more planned for you!

Sometimes, people have approached the baptism in the Holy Spirit as the completion of something. They pray for it. They receive it. They experience the first miracle of praying in a spiritual language, but that's the finale for them. They stop seeking more of God's power. They stop expecting more miracles to be released into their lives. What a shame. This experience was never designed to be an end in and of itself; it was always designed to be the beginning of a powerful spiritual life.

It's the starting point for living out a supernatural life.

QUESTION 5:
WHAT DOES SPEAKING IN TONGUES HAVE TO DO WITH THE BAPTISM IN THE HOLY SPIRIT? CAN'T I JUST BE FILLED WITH THE SPIRIT WITHOUT THAT?

The real question is this: Why do you want to be baptized in the Holy Spirit? Do you just want to say that it happened for you? Do you want to cross it off the list of things you have experienced in life? Do you just want to feel better about yourself that you have attained a certain spiritual plateau and don't need anything more?

Or are you seeking to live a supernatural life? Do you want power to be a witness of the resurrection of Jesus? Do you want to be a vessel Jesus can use to deliver His miracles to broken and needy people? Are you hungry to know the full release of the river of the Holy Spirit in your life? Do you want to feel the rush of His presence, purpose, and power unleashed through you?

If you want a supernatural life, then you need to think of speaking in tongues as the first miracle that He will do through you. Why is this the first? Why can't He do other miracles with me first? Why does it have to be this?

The Bible gives a list of nine miraculous ways that God uses believers. It's found in 1 Corinthians 12 and it involves things like: gifts of healing, word of wisdom, words of knowledge, prophecy, and faith. The Spirit of God distributes these gifts to each believer as He determines for the common good of the entire body of Christ.

Yet He begins with the baptism in the Holy Spirit and the language-miracle of speaking in tongues for several reasons:

- *It's personal*—no one else has to be there. It's just you and the Holy Spirit. All you have to do to see this miracle is to speak out the words that He gives you to say.
- *It's a partnership*—since speaking in tongues involves just you and the Holy Spirit, as you pray in your spiritual language, you practice a partnership with the Holy Spirit. Every time you pray in tongues, you are practicing what it is to operate in the supernatural. You are tuning in to His voice. You are speaking out what you have heard in the Spirit. These are all the skills you will need when He uses you in a public fashion.

- *It's powerful*—every time you speak in tongues, the strength of the Holy Spirit is released within you. This gives power to your inner being. Paul described it like this, "Anyone who speaks in a tongue edifies [builds up and adds strength to] themselves" (1 Corinthians 14:4).

So this practice of praying in the Spirit is something that becomes a gateway to a supernatural life. The Holy Spirit is released in your inner being, and His power comes out through your lips, before it comes out in your life.

DISCUSSION QUESTIONS FOR CHAPTER FOUR

1. When you first heard of speaking in tongues, what was your reaction?
2. Have you ever felt undue pressure to do something, spiritually, that perhaps you weren't ready to do? What effect did that have on you?
3. What is the right motive to pursue any significant experience with God? What are some wrong motives?
4. Read Romans 8:26–28. What is the role of the Holy Spirit in your prayer life and in fulfilling God's purpose for your life?
5. What next steps are you going to take to give the Holy Spirit a more active role in the way you pray?

CHAPTER FIVE

IT'S PRAYERFUL!

In the same way, the Spirit helps us in our weakness. We do not know what
we ought to pray for, but the Spirit himself intercedes for us through wordless
groans. And he who searches our hearts knows the mind of the Spirit, because
the Spirit intercedes for God's people in accordance with the will of God
(ROMANS 8:26–27).

A little over a decade ago, a man named Bashar lived with his
family in Iraq. As the atmosphere in that nation grew more
dangerous, he knew it was time to move his family out of harm's
way. So he found a place for his wife and kids to stay in Syria. After
getting them settled, Bashar made his way to Sweden, where he
could apply for refugee status, attempt to get a job, and prepare to
bring his family with him to Sweden.

Shortly after arriving in Sweden, Bashar met Johannes Amritzer
on a subway train. Johannes shared the message of Christ with
Bashar and invited him to attend church in Stockholm. Before long,
Bashar made the decision to give his life to Christ. He was baptized
in water and a while later was baptized in the Holy Spirit.

Every day Bashar grew in his faith. Every day he prayed for his wife
and kids who were living thousands of miles away. Johannes had taught
him the value of praying in tongues, and Bashar practiced this on a
regular basis. When he entered his prayer time, he began by praying in
his native language of Arabic. Then as he worshipped God, he would
speak out the syllables he felt the Holy Spirit inspired him to say.

Soon this practice of praying in the Spirit became more than
comfortable to him. He was tuning into the Holy Spirit's operation

within his heart. He was speaking out in faith what he sensed the Holy Spirit prompted within. As he did this, he felt stronger and in the flow of the Holy Spirit's work within him.

One day, Bashar received a call from his wife. Life was becoming increasingly dangerous in Syria, so she wanted to take the children across the border back into Iraq. She felt that going back to live with friends, in the neighborhood she knew best, would be the safest option. Bashar asked her to remain where she was until he had the chance to think and pray about this idea.

Bashar recounts, "Something inside of me didn't feel right about the move. So I began to pour out my heart to God in prayer. In Farsi, I prayed for God to give me direction and to protect my family. But somehow, that didn't seem to be enough. So I began to pray in my spiritual language." Throughout the day Bashar prayed in the Spirit for his wife and children and whether they should leave Syria and return to Iraq.

Suddenly, God spoke to him clearly as he prayed in tongues. A strong inner sense of warning said, "Do not let your wife go back to Iraq." As Bashar continued to pray, the inner impression grew stronger and stronger. So he picked up the phone and called his wife. "I feel that you must not leave Syria. You must stay where you are." She responded, "But I don't feel safe here. I have already made calls and arranged for us to go, and we are preparing to leave right now." Bashar insisted urgently, "I am your husband, and you and the children mean everything to me. I must insist that you stay in Syria. Please don't go to Iraq under any circumstance."

Then he explained to her what had happened as he prayed. He told her that the Holy Spirit had warned him about the dangers in Iraq. Even though it seemed a logical move to leave Syria, God had said his wife was to stay in Syria. When she heard his explanation, she agreed to remain where she was for at least a few more weeks.

Two days later, a suicide bomber detonated an explosive in the neighborhood in Iraq where she would have been staying. The room in the apartment building his family would have been sleeping in was completely destroyed. Had his wife crossed the border and returned

> Most often, the use of a spiritual language is to assist us to pray as the Holy Spirit prays through us.

to Iraq, she and the children would have died in that explosion.

When I first met Bashar in Sweden, he recounted this story to me. Then he added, "Pastor, you must teach everyone you know about the baptism in the Holy Spirit. I pray in tongues all the time. Praying in the Spirit saved my family. It's the best gift I have ever received."

In the previous chapter, we discussed the initial miracle that occurs when we are baptized in the Holy Spirit. We begin to speak out (pray) in a language we have never studied or learned. This is a language miracle. We call this "praying in tongues," or "praying in the Spirit," or I have used the phrase "praying in my spiritual language."

The Bible records two uses for this language miracle:

1. *Prayer*: The primary purpose is a private and personal one. Most often, the use of a spiritual language is to assist us to pray as the Holy Spirit prays through us. We will discuss this use of the language miracle throughout the rest of this chapter.

2. *Proclamation*: The second purpose is a public one. The book of First Corinthians, chapters 12 and 14, mentions two spiritual gifts that almost always work together in a public setting: tongues and the interpretation of tongues.

Tongues, then, are a sign, not for believers but for unbelievers. (1 Corinthians 14:22)

If anyone speaks in a tongue, two—or at the most three—should speak, one at a time, and someone

> must interpret. If there is no interpreter, the
> speaker should keep quiet in the church and speak
> to himself and to God. (1 Corinthians 14:27–28)

Here Paul gave instructions to the church at Corinth as to how spiritual gifts should operate in their public gatherings. He outlined the purpose for the combination of tongues and interpretation. Tongues served as a "sign" for unbelievers. How so? It is a bilingual miracle. If a person entered the public service and heard someone speak supernaturally in the hearer's native language, and then heard another person supernaturally interpret that message, that would be a pretty convincing sign that God was at work!

But the governing rules are these: Speaking in tongues has no value in a public service unless it is accompanied by an interpretation and therefore is used as a sign to a specific unbeliever that God is at work. Notice what Paul says in verse 28. If no interpreter is present, the one speaking in tongues should keep quiet in the church (the public place of use) and should speak only to himself and to God (using tongues in prayer).

We see that there are two uses for the spiritual language: one is public and one is private. One use is for proclamation; the other use is for private prayer. Many believers will never use tongues publicly to proclaim a message that will be supernaturally interpreted. But everyone can expect to use tongues personally and in prayer. Notice how the apostle Paul described his own experience:

> I thank God that I speak in tongues more than all
> of you [privately and in prayer]. But in the church
> [publicly and to proclaim] I would rather speak
> five intelligible words to instruct others than ten
> thousand words in a tongue. (1 Corinthians 14:18–19)

So what are the benefits of speaking in tongues in your personal prayer life?

INTERCESSION

The word *intercession* means "to plead or advocate on behalf of another." This is what the Holy Spirit does for us when we pray in our spiritual language. He uses our lips and our voice to pray accurately, powerfully, and effectively to God about a situation of great importance. The Holy Spirit interceded through Bashar for his family members who were in grave danger.

> In the same way, the Spirit helps us in our weakness. We do not know what we ought to pray for, but the Spirit himself intercedes for us through wordless groans. And he who searches our hearts knows the mind of the Spirit, because the Spirit intercedes for God's people in accordance with the will of God. (Romans 8:26–27)

- *Our prayers need help.* Often we don't know what to pray for. Some situations are so complicated that we don't even know where to begin. The Spirit helps us in our weakness and intercedes through us. He knows exactly what we need to pray.
- *Our prayers lack accuracy.* When we pray, we are uncertain as to what God's will is in a specific situation. But the "Spirit intercedes . . . in accordance with the will of God." He knows exactly what God's will is.
- *Our prayers require expression.* Often words simply aren't enough. At times we feel so burdened in our spirits that saying words into the air seems incomplete. But the Spirit helps us carry that inner burden to the Lord. The Holy Spirit groans along with us until our need has been carried into the heavens and deposited in the hands of God.

As a young boy, I remember hearing the phrase, "praying through." Someone would say, "I need to pray through about this." They meant, "I need to pray in the Spirit until the burden I feel in my spirit lifts off of me." When we feel a heaviness in our spirits about something, it often feels like a weight on our chest. Praying in the Spirit is a way of gradually pushing that weight off of us and onto the shoulders of the Lord.

> The Holy Spirit groans along with us until our need has been carried into the heavens and deposited in the hands of God.

EDIFICATION

Edification is defined as "being uplifted, strengthened, and inwardly benefited." The passage in 1 Corinthians 14 provides so much insight into this practice of praying in the Spirit. One of the benefits listed is that of personal edification. Every time I pray in the Spirit, I feel uplifted, and strengthened in my spirit. Let's break down the specifics in these verses:

1. Speaking in tongues helps us talk to God.

> *For anyone who speaks in a tongue does not speak to people but to God. (1 Corinthians 14:2)*

2. When I speak in tongues, I don't understand what I'm saying. I let the Holy Spirit talk to God through me directly to the Father.

> *Indeed, no one understands them [the person speaking in tongues]; they utter mysteries by the Spirit. (1 Corinthians 14:2)*

3. Prophecy is the public gift that has the most value because it's a clear way of speaking understandable words that edify those who hear them. Prophecy strengthens, encourages, and comforts others.

> *But the one who prophesies speaks to people for their strengthening, encouraging and comfort.*
> *(1 Corinthians 14:3)*

4. When I speak in tongues, I edify myself. I'm speaking in a way that strengthens, encourages, and comforts my own soul.

> *Anyone who speaks in a tongue edifies themselves, but the one who prophesies edifies the church.*
> *(1 Corinthians 14:4)*

5. Everyone would benefit by praying in tongues.

> *I would like every one of you to speak in tongues. . . .*
> *(1 Corinthians 14:5)*

A few years ago, my dear friend Bruce Edwards was in a swimming accident off the coast of Delaware. Bruce was knocked off his feet by a wave, hit the ocean floor with his head, and was instantly paralyzed. By the time he reached the hospital, after being life-flighted from the coast, his brain had been severely impaired. For ten days, Bruce was in the ICU in a hospital in Philadelphia. My wife and I made the drive across Pennsylvania at least four times during that ten-day period. Not only was Bruce a close friend of almost thirty years, he was a pastor on my staff.

Many times during those difficult days I didn't know what or how to pray. I felt shocked, confused, depleted, and empty. But I knew I needed to provide strength and presence to Bruce's family during this season as they stood by his bedside during those critical moments. So I prayed in the Spirit.

There are two practices that have a similar effect on my soul. I feel stronger inside when I worship. I feel stronger inside when I pray in tongues. Worship lifts my spirit because I invite and step into the presence of God. Praying in tongues is a release to my spirit because this lifts the weight on my heart and deposits it into the care of God. It provides

> Praying as prompted by the Holy Spirit is an offensive weapon in spiritual warfare.

peace and release. As I traveled back and forth to the hospital, I spent the time worshipping and praying in tongues. This made me stronger in every way.

When I prayed in the Spirit during those moments in ICU, I felt the Holy Spirit release everything I needed. He gave me peace that surpassed my understanding, strength to minister to the family, and the ability to access the resources of His grace in those moments of tremendous need.

CONFRONTATION

Confrontation is the act of opposing groups clashing with one another and challenging each other. The Bible declares that we are in a place of constant confrontation with the forces of darkness. Ephesians 6:10–13 challenges us: "Be strong in the Lord and in his mighty power . . . so that you can take your stand against the devil's schemes. For our struggle is not against flesh and blood, but against the rulers, against the authorities, against the powers of this dark world and against the spiritual forces of evil in the heavenly realms."

Following this challenge is a list of ways we need to prepare ourselves for this ongoing and constant fight. It involves wearing spiritual armor much like a gladiator or Roman soldier would have worn: a helmet, a breastplate, a belt, shoes/shin guards, a sword, and a shield. The sword is compared to how we use God's Word. It's sharp and cuts through the lies and deceptions of the Devil and his dark attempts to destroy us.

> In addition to all this, take up the shield of faith with which you can extinguish all the flaming arrows of the evil one. Take the helmet of salvation and the sword of the Spirit, which is the word of God. And *pray in the spirit on all occasions* with all kinds of prayers and requests. With this in mind, be alert and keep on praying for all the Lord's people. (Ephesians 6:16–18, emphasis added)

Praying as prompted by the Holy Spirit is an offensive weapon in spiritual warfare. As we pray in our spiritual language, we are not only pushing the weight off of our spirits, we are pushing against the current of darkness.

I think the best illustration of what spiritual warfare feels like is the current that you feel when you walk out into the ocean. Every few steps, a wave crashes against your body. You have to stand strong to keep from being pushed over. The current not only tries to push you back, it tends to drag you down the shore. If you aren't careful, the ocean current will pull you down shore when you think you are standing still. You have to pay attention constantly to how the push of the waters is affecting you.

The Devil sends a spiritual current against your life every day. If you aren't aware, it can knock you over. If you aren't vigilant, it can carry you to a place you don't want to go. If you want to go somewhere positive with your life, you have to push intentionally against the current to gain new ground at a better place.

Praying in the Spirit helps us push against that current. Actually, praying in the Spirit creates a counter current. The power of the Holy Spirit releases a new wave within you that is headed in the opposite direction. God begins to push against the darkness through you. The Holy Spirit is released like the blowing of a new wind that will carry you over the rough waters and into a place where you are sailing over the attacks against your life.

FORTIFICATION

Fortification has to do with making something stronger by rooting it deeply into a relationship with something or someone else. When we pray in the Holy Spirit, we are connected and established in our relationship with Christ. "But you, dear friends, by building yourself up in your most holy faith, and *praying in the Holy Spirit*, keep yourself in God's love as you wait for the mercy of our Lord Jesus Christ to bring you to eternal life" (Jude 20–21, emphasis added).

1. *The Holy Spirit establishes us in God's love*. He reveals the fact that God never stops loving us, no matter what. When we pray in the Spirit, the Holy Spirit reminds us that we are adopted and accepted by God.

2. *The Holy Spirit reminds us of truth*. Jesus said in John 16:13, "When he, the Spirit of truth, comes, he will guide you into all the truth." Praying in the Spirit affirms, confirms, and unlocks the truths in the Scripture.

3. *The Holy Spirit strengthens our faith*. As we pray in the Spirit our capacity to believe what God has promised increases. The Holy Spirit possesses all the faith and all the power that we need. As He operates within us, more and more of what He has, becomes available to us.

REVELATION

Revelation is defined as "making something evident" or "disclosing that which is hidden." We will devote the entire next chapter to this benefit of praying in the Spirit. Many times we need to know something that is hidden from us. God knows, but we don't know. As we pray in tongues, the Holy Spirit reveals things we could never know otherwise.

Bashar experienced a revelation from God. As he prayed in the Holy Spirit, God impressed on his mind that danger lurked in Iraq, where his family wanted to go. Logically, it seemed less dangerous than where they were staying in Syria. But the Holy Spirit knew the facts. He knew that on a particular day, at a specific time, an explosion would destroy the very apartment where Bashar's wife and family would be. This revelation from the Holy Spirit preserved their lives.

This is the kind of experience we can expect when we are baptized in the Holy Spirit. The next chapter is all about just how much God can reveal into your life.

DISCUSSION QUESTIONS FOR CHAPTER FIVE

1. Have you ever participated in an activity that required accuracy? For example, firing a bow and arrow or throwing darts? What are some of the keys to accuracy?

2. Why is the Holy Spirit more accurate than we are when it comes to praying according to the will of God?

3. Research tells us that there is an after-effect to exercise. Endorphins are released into your system after a workout, which leaves you feeling a rush of energy and emotion. They call this a "runner's high." In a similar way, praying in the Holy Spirit edifies your inner spirit. How does that work, in your opinion?

4. Have you ever felt that God spoke by the Holy Spirit into your life? Can you describe how that worked and what it was like?

5. What can you do this week to position yourself to hear from God in a greater way?

CHAPTER SIX

IT'S REVELATIONAL!

"When we pray in the Spirit, the Bible says that we pray mysteries with
our spirit unto God. Usually we don't know what we are praying about, but the
Spirit knows and prays for us according to God's will. And God is a reciprocal
God. As we pray mysteries with our spirit, the pipeline of heaven is open
and God reveals mysteries back to us as well."

—RON JOHNSON, PASTOR
ONE CHURCH, ORLANDO, FL

I t was October of 2012. Ron Johnson had traveled from his home
in Orlando, Florida, to attend a pastor's roundtable in Huntsville,
Alabama. All the participants checked into the hotel and made
their way down to dinner. After the first day of meetings was
over, Ron began to feel a deep uneasiness in his spirit. Something
wasn't right.

So he retreated to his room and began to pray in the Spirit, seeking
God for the reason why he felt so disturbed. First Corinthians 12
describes various expressions or manifestations of the Holy Spirit's
supernatural work through the life of a believer. Several of the
gifts mentioned there are for the purpose of revelation; when God
discloses something to a believer at the moment of a specific need.

- A word of knowledge is a supernatural revelation of a fact
  or detail about a person or situation.
- A word of wisdom is a supernatural revelation of direction
  or application in providing wise and sound counsel as to
  what to do in a situation.

- Discerning of spirits is the supernatural revelation of what specific spirit is at work in a situation (the human spirit, a demonic spirit, or the Holy Spirit).

When a person is baptized in the Holy Spirit, they become sensitized to these kinds of supernatural disclosures from God. So Ron prayed in tongues, and his spirit became even more receptive to what the Holy Spirit was saying to him. As he prayed, he felt a strong urging to leave Huntsville immediately. That was all the information he received.

> The Holy Spirit knows the Father's will, and He prays through us in accordance with God's will.

When God grants revelation about something, He doesn't always explain Himself thoroughly or provide all the details. He gives us everything we need to know to take the next step and make the right decision. Often, He won't let us rest until we have acted upon His guidance. Ron knew he couldn't stay in Huntsville. So he began the series of awkward conversations about leaving early.

He called his wife and said, "Please change my plane ticket. I want to leave right away." He explained to his colleagues that he felt unrest and needed to leave immediately. They were surprised but supported his decision. He checked out of the hotel, traveled to the airport, and stayed the night at a hotel near the airport so he could fly out to Orlando the next day.

During the night, a tornado blew through Huntsville, Alabama. It touched down just outside the hotel where the roundtable was being held. It struck the hotel that night, and the point of impact was the very room where Ron had been staying. If Ron had remained, he would most likely have been killed. The other pastors attending the conference were staying several floors below. When they heard the warnings, they crawled under the staircase in the hallway next to their rooms and successfully weathered the storm without injury.

As Ron flew out the next morning, he was thanking God for the gift of the Holy Spirit in his life and for the protection God provided through the supernatural disclosure (or revelation) of the Holy Spirit.

Ron Johnson is the pastor of One Church in Orlando, Florida. I have heard him teach a rather unique concept about how praying in tongues makes us more sensitive to the information the Holy Spirit wants to give to us. First Corinthians 14:2 teaches us this, "Anyone who speaks in a tongue does not speak to people but to God. Indeed, no one understands them; they utter mysteries by the Spirit."

The Holy Spirit prays through us. The Holy Spirit understands what He is praying through our lips, but we don't know the specifics. When we pray in tongues, we often have a burden for a person or a situation, but we don't know exactly what the Spirit of God is praying through us for them; we are uttering "mysteries by the Spirit."

Again, in Romans 8:26–27 we read, "We do not know what we ought to pray for, but the Spirit himself intercedes for us through wordless groans. And he who searches our hearts knows the mind of the Spirit, because the Spirit intercedes for God's people in accordance with the will of God." The Father searches our hearts and knows the mind of the Spirit. The Holy Spirit knows the Father's will, and He prays through us in accordance with God's will.

So here's what we can deduce from these verses:

1. Praying in the Spirit opens the pipeline of communication between the Holy Spirit within us and God the Father in heaven.
2. The Spirit of God groans out (utters) prayers according to God's will through us. They are mysteries to us, and yet they are precisely what needs to be prayed at the moment to meet the needs of that specific situation.
3. Since the pipeline of communication is open as we pray in this way, we are more ready to receive mysteries/revelation of what the Father would like to disclose to us.

Ron Johnson teaches, "God is a reciprocal God. When we allow the Holy Spirit to speak mysteries to the Father, through us—the Father then responds by revealing mysteries to our spirits as well."

Praying in the Spirit sensitizes us to the voice of God. It makes us more aware of His leadings and His promptings. Praying in the Spirit heightens the sensitivity of the "nervous system" in your spirit. Just as certain conditions and treatments can give the nerves in your skin a heightened sensitivity to touch, so praying in the Spirit provides us with a heightened sensitivity in the spiritual realm. We hear things in the Spirit much more clearly than we would otherwise.

I know this probably isn't the best example, but stay with me on this one: "Dogs have a very acute sense of hearing. While their sense of smell ranks first, their hearing is not too far behind. Canines hear much better than humans do; over four times greater to be precise. . . . [One] reason is that the frequencies that dogs hear are much higher and lower than what humans can hear. Dogs hear a frequency range of 40 to 60,000 Hz while a human range is between 20 and 20,000 Hz."[5]

Somehow, praying in the Spirit increases the frequency range of our spiritual ears. We are more tuned it to the interaction between the Holy Spirit within us and the message that heaven is trying to send us.

This may be one of the reasons why the baptism in the Holy Spirit becomes a gateway to the other gifts of the Spirit mentioned in 1 Corinthians 12. Remember, the purpose of the baptism in the Holy Spirit is to clothe you with power. This explosive capacity from God is designed to help you testify to the fact that Jesus has risen from the dead. The miracles God releases through you are confirming signs that prove He is alive and working in the world.

Speaking in tongues occurs at the moment we are baptized in the Holy Spirit. It's a "starter" gift that is the gateway for us to begin to function in the supernatural power of God. How so?

- *Speaking in tongues is the easiest gift to function in regularly:* When we pray in tongues, we are functioning in the supernatural in our personal and private prayer life. The

Holy Spirit is talking to God through us with His words and His concepts.

- *Speaking in tongues makes us more sensitive in our spirits:* As the channels of communication open up between heaven and earth, our spirits become more tuned in to what God is saying and doing in the world. Being sensitive to the promptings of the Holy Spirit is a major key to functioning in the other gifts.

For instance, one of the gifts of the Spirit (1 Corinthians 12:7–10) is the gift of healing. When I pray for someone to be healed, it helps if I can hear the Holy Spirit tell me who to pray for and what specifically God intends to do for them. Another gift of the Spirit is the gift of prophecy. Prophecy, in its simplest definition, is Holy Spirit-inspired encouragement. We speak words to build up, lift up, and bind up those who need fresh encouragement. Prophecy is directed toward a person and their unique need. How can we prophesy/speak out something that we have not first of all heard/sensed within our spirits?

If you examine the gifts of the Spirit, each one requires "hearing" from the Holy Spirit before acting in faith based on what we hear.

Speaking in tongues provides a way for me to practice hearing and obeying. When I hear the syllables in my spirit and speak them in prayer, I'm doing the very thing that I do in any of the other supernatural gifts: God speaks, I hear, I obey, and God acts.

The purpose is clear for the baptism in the Holy Spirit. God wants you to live a supernatural life. He wants to give you power to testify of His resurrection. He wants you to eagerly desire to be used in the gifts of the Spirit (1 Corinthians 14:1). Many believers in the western world have argued that the baptism in the Holy Spirit isn't necessary today. Some have said that the baptism in the Holy Spirit should be sought, but that speaking in tongues isn't necessary. Others believe that all these things (tongues, spiritual gifts, miracles) ceased when the original apostles died. They teach that miracles no longer occur in the life of the believer.

I find all of these arguments fall short of what we actually read in the Scriptures and by what I know from experience.

First of all, why would Jesus make this the final thing He said to His disciples, if He didn't intend for the baptism in the Holy Spirit to be important? Remember, this was what Jesus commanded just before He ascended into heaven. How could that command not be perceived as critically important to the mission He had assigned to them?

Second, in the New Testament, every time believers were baptized in the Holy Spirit, supernatural things began to happen. They spoke in tongues. They prophesied. They prayed for the sick and people were healed. The entirety of the book of Acts is a history of the miraculous work of the Holy Spirit through the life of the believer. Has God suddenly stopped working in this way?

> Perhaps we should be so hungry to see the power of God released in our generation that we're willing to do whatever we need to do to be used by Him in His power.

Third, since over half of the world doesn't know Jesus as their Savior, why would God cease providing proof of His resurrection? Don't Muslims need to know that Jesus is the Son of God, risen from the dead? Don't Hindus need more than words to believe? Don't atheists deserve more than moralistic philosophy and/or stories of the power of God that are nearly 2,000 years old?

It suggests to me that perhaps we shouldn't spend so much time figuring out how to operate in the supernatural power of God without having to speak in tongues. Perhaps, instead, we should step boldly into what Jesus commanded His disciples to receive and exercise. Perhaps we should be so hungry to see the power of God released in our generation that we're willing to do whatever we need to do to be used by Him in His power. Perhaps we should so long to see people come to Christ that we're willing to be used as vessels for God to testify to the world of Jesus' resurrection.

A PERSONAL EXPERIENCE

A few years ago, I had a dream. I had just returned from an overseas festival in Africa where we preached the gospel to an unreached people group that had never heard the gospel before. During that week of meetings, I spent a lot of time praying in the Spirit to prepare myself for the ministry that would happen during the festival gatherings. The atmosphere of the meetings was charged with Holy Spirit power; many deaf ears were opened and blind eyes began to see.

My spiritual nervous system was a bit more tuned up than normal, and that sensitivity showed up in one of my dreams. In Acts 2, Simon Peter refers to a prophecy in the book of Joel (written several hundred years earlier) about the outpouring of the Holy Spirit: "In the last days, God says, I will pour out my Spirit on all people. Your sons and daughters will prophesy, your old men will dream dreams, your young men will see visions" (Joel 2:28).

This is what happened for me. In my dream, I was standing in the fellowship space (we call it our concourse) at Allison Park Church. There were five or six others standing with me in a circle, and next to me was a tall blonde woman I didn't recognize. As we were standing there and talking, this woman bent over in pain and seemed to be manifesting a demonic spirit. In the Bible we read about people possessed by demons and how they act out in a way that seems almost beyond their control. This is what was happening in my dream.

When I saw her react this way, I turned to her and spoke. I heard myself saying, "In Jesus' name, come out!" But nothing happened. She continued to manifest this demon as my prayers over her were unsuccessful. In a split second, I was awake. But the dream was still vivid in my mind. In fact, it disturbed me quite a bit. If you have ever found yourself awake after a scary dream, you know this experience of going from a dream state to being really awake. I was trembling and sweating. My adrenaline was pumping, and I knew it would be impossible to go right back to sleep.

So I got up and began to pray. I asked God, "Who is this woman? Why did I have this dream about her? More importantly, why did the demon not come out when I used the name of Jesus?" This was actually very disturbing to me. So I began to pray in the Spirit. I recalled this teaching from Ron Johnson that praying in the Spirit makes us ready to hear from God more clearly.

I paced back and forth in my living room, praying in my spiritual language. It was 3:30 a.m., but I was wide awake and felt a burden for this woman's situation whoever she was. As I prayed in tongues, I replayed in my mind the scene from my dream. When I did, the scene shifted. All of the sudden, I saw this same blonde woman, sitting in the corner, crying, rocking back and forth, and holding onto a necklace of some type.

Remember, I was awake at this point, but I was seeing this scene in my mind much like a movie being played for me. To distinguish what was happening, we would say that I was having a "vision" from God. A vision is simply a dream we have when we're awake. A dream can be a vision from God that we get when we are sleeping. Not all dreams are from God. But I knew that this one was.

I stopped praying in the Spirit for a moment, and I asked God, "Why has she not been set free? What is she holding onto as she cries? What needs to happen next?" I stopped praying for a season, and I sang to God in worship. Then I returned to prayer and prayed in my spiritual language as I again tuned into this vision. I heard the Holy Spirit say to me, "The necklace she is wearing is the key. She is holding onto this, and what it represents is keeping her bound. If you get her to surrender the necklace, she will be set free."

Then, in the Spirit, I saw that happen. She took off the necklace, stood to her feet, threw her hands in the air, and worshipped God because she was finally free of what had tormented her for so long. I felt a sense of relief and release. I knew that I had heard from God.

This all happened on a Saturday night, and I had a sense that this woman might show up at church the next day. I woke up my wife, Melodie, and explained the dream to her. I'll never forget the look on her face as she rubbed her eyes and tried to figure out why her husband had seemingly gone crazy in the middle of the night.

Then I said to her, "This woman might come to church tomorrow. Since I'm speaking tomorrow, you might have to minister to her if she starts to manifest these demons during the message. If she does, here is what you are supposed to do." I explained to her the significance of the necklace. I told her, "The necklace is the key; you have to get her to give up the necklace." Needless to say, Melodie was a bit unnerved but was willing to deal with the situation if it arose.

Sunday morning, just before the start of the service, I was standing in the café in our concourse. As I turned, I saw a tall blonde woman enter the building. It was the woman I had seen in my dream. I turned to my wife and said, "That's her! That's the woman I saw in my dream." So my wife went over and began to visit with the woman. Melodie welcomed her to church, and they got to know one another.

I went into the service and began to lead and prepare to speak. While my wife continued to talk with the woman, the woman bent over as if she was in pain. (Yes, it was just like I had seen in the dream). She told my wife, "I think I'm going to be sick." Melodie led her to a private space where the blonde woman could catch her breath and they could talk and pray. Melodie prayed for her and every time she said the name of Jesus, the woman seemed to get worse. She groaned and bent over as Melodie mentioned Jesus' name. It was obvious that a demonic spirit was affecting the woman's life.

After a season of prayer and conversation, Melodie remembered my instructions: "You have to get her to remove that necklace because something about that necklace is keeping her bound." So my wife inquired about the necklace, "I notice that when you bend over you hold onto your necklace. Does that necklace mean something to you?" The woman replied, "Yes, my boyfriend gave it to me. He abused me sexually, physically, and emotionally, and just recently left me. I feel so used and alone. So I sit in the corner in my apartment and I cry and hold onto this necklace as a way of remembering him and what he did to me."

Melodie responded, "Would you be willing to give me that necklace? And as you give it to me, you need to choose to let your boyfriend go. Turn your heart over to God. Let God heal the pain inside. He wants to set you free, but you have to choose to surrender to Him and let Jesus restore your soul."

"Yes," the woman responded, "I'll give you the necklace. I probably should give you the bracelets as well, because he gave these to me also." So she took them off one at a time and placed them in Melodie's hands. Then she prayed the salvation prayer and gave her life to Jesus Christ. As soon as she finished the prayer, she stood up and lifted her hands to God. Tears were streaming down her face as the inner healing process began.

Jesus set her free just like I saw in the dream!

This is why the baptism in the Holy Spirit is so important. Through the infilling of the Holy Spirit, God gives us access to information and revelation that we would never have in any other way. He loved that woman so much that He went to the trouble to wake me up with a dream about her plight. As I prayed in the Spirit, He unfolded to me the words of knowledge I needed to provide the pathway out of her torment. As the service continued that morning, the Holy Spirit ministered to this woman as He worked through Melodie to lead her to a place of freedom.

God wants to use **you** to impact people by the power of God. He wants to speak to you and through you. He wants to work miracles through your prayers. He wants to release healing and freedom through you. Because the Holy Spirit lives within you, you have the potential to do anything that God asks you to do. The Holy Spirit wants to do miracles through you.

All of this is possible when we are clothed with power; when we receive the fire clothes of Jesus through the baptism in the Holy Spirit.

DISCUSSION QUESTIONS FOR CHAPTER SIX

1. Have you ever seen a dog respond to a dog whistle? Is it hard for you to believe the dog can hear something that you can't?
2. Is it possible for you to become a little more sensitive to some sounds rather than others? (Example: Moms are sensitive to the cries of their newborns). Can you think of other examples?
3. What makes us most sensitive to the voice of the Holy Spirit? How do you know that you are hearing His voice?
4. What's the weirdest dream you have ever had? Read Acts 2:17–18. Have you ever had God speak to you in a dream or a vision?
5. How can we be more aware and open to what God wants to communicate with us this week?

CHAPTER SEVEN

IT'S RELEVANT!

The cause of weakness in your Christian life is that you want to work it out
partly, and let God help you. And that cannot be. You must become utterly
helpless, to let God work, and God will work gloriously.[6]
—ANDREW MURRAY

B ack in the 1990s, it was our practice at Allison Park Church to hold
a Sunday night service. Sunday nights were different from our
normal Sunday morning services. They were designed for people to
spend extra time in worship and in prayer. We gave a teaching, but the
atmosphere was designed for people to have an experience with God.

One Sunday night, Leah Ferguson was teaching. As she gave
the message, she paused and shared a "word of knowledge." Now
remember that the baptism in the Holy Spirit is the gateway to
living a supernatural life. As a person learns to partner with the Holy
Spirit, they start to function in the various gifts of the Holy Spirit
that are described in 1 Corinthians 12:7-10. One of those gifts is
the word of knowledge, which is the revelation to a person of a fact
about someone or something that could not be known naturally.

Leah said, "Someone is here tonight who has experienced deep pain.
God is getting ready to heal you in that area. As you humble yourself
before Him, He is going to touch that area of pain and scarring and
begin complete healing in that area of your life." After she said this, she
went on with her teaching and none of us thought anything about it.

In the audience that night was a man by the name of Kevin
Kuchta. Kevin had been attending Allison Park Church for only a few
months. He had a physical condition that caused him to experience

pain in his bones. The bone disease, Avascular Necrosis, was caused by medicine he received for an intestinal disease. The medication actually caused major portions of his femurs to die, leaving the surviving bone to become stressed, brittle, and susceptible to fracture. He had undergone multiple surgeries to address the disease in his legs, and yet the problem had not been corrected. Modern medicine can do many incredible things, but it can't bring tissue back from the dead. He had deep pain and physical scarring because of the condition and many orthopedic surgeries.

The most obvious way you could see the physical impact on Kevin was that he couldn't get around without either a wheelchair or crutches. When Kevin heard the word of knowledge from Leah, something inside of him began to burn. The Holy Spirit spoke to him and said, "That word was for you!"

So at the end of the service, Kevin responded to Leah's altar call. He used his crutches to get himself to the front of the auditorium. He did what was requested in the word of knowledge. He humbled himself. He recounts that he doesn't remember how he got down on the floor. Usually, that would take help from someone, someone strong.

There Kevin lay facedown before the Lord. "Then it happened. I felt the power of God come all over me. It was so strong that I began to tremble violently. My entire body would shake for a season, and then it would subside. Then again, it would come on me like a wave. I would shake, and then it would subside. This happened about ten to twelve times. I was scared, but I kept hearing, *Be still and know that I am God.* On the final time, I felt a searing pain in my back right where my kidneys are located. When the pain stopped, I felt a sense of peace."

Kevin felt God speaking to him again. "Stand up!" Kevin argued, "But God, I'm not sure how I can get up off the floor without help. It's impossible for me to do this." Again, Kevin sensed that inner voice of the Holy Spirit telling him to stand. So he obeyed. He pushed himself to his knees, then he tried to get from his knees to his feet. To his surprise, his legs held his weight without pain and with free range of motion. He stood straight up.

I was standing at the front of the auditorium talking to another person. Almost everyone had departed because it was about thirty minutes after the service had ended. Kevin was new to me as he was new to the church. When I saw him standing there, I said, "Hi, Kevin." It didn't dawn on me that he was standing without crutches since I didn't know him that well.

He said to me, "Hey, Pastor Jeff! Look at me! I am standing right here!" "Yes," I said, "I can see that," not really sure what in the world he meant. Then Kevin pointed to his crutches that were lying on the floor. "I'm standing here!" Kevin explained as he saw my obvious confusion. I asked, "What happened? Did you experience a healing miracle?" "I think so!" Kevin responded in a sort of shock-and-awe moment.

He said that he was scared. I didn't understand why until he said, "What if this isn't real? If this is just adrenaline or something, and I tried to walk, I could break my leg. My left femur has fractured in the past just by moving myself on my living room couch." He was confused and scared. I asked him what exactly happened. As he told me, he realized that it just had to be what it indeed was, a miracle! Then it really dawned on us both. What a moment and what a mixture of emotions. Joy! Tears! Laughter! Shock! Gratitude! It was quite a way to end a Sunday night service!

Kevin picked up his crutches and carried them out the back door. I will never ever forget that moment. It was a genuine verifiable, supernatural event that had happened right in our church! And it happened as a result of the Holy Spirit working in the life of one person to prompt a miracle in the life of another.

By the way, Kevin is a scientist. He normally rolled into work in his wheelchair. You can imagine the impact of his life when he walked into work on Monday morning: no wheelchair, no crutches, healed. The scientists had no explanation for what had happened to Kevin, but they could see visible proof that Jesus is alive and is still doing miracles in the world today. I asked Kevin to follow up with his doctors. Later, he told me that his surgeons examined him and were amazed. The chief surgeon, after examining his range of motion and comparative x-rays, looked at him and said, "Sometimes you just have to call a miracle, a 'miracle'!"

I just described for you one of the most amazing instances I have ever seen of the Holy Spirit's work through the life of a surrendered believer. If every story we heard about the Holy Spirit ended this way, there would never be anything controversial whatsoever about this experience. But not everyone has had an experience like Kevin's. Some have been in a room where someone expressed a spiritual gift and it was either weird, awkward, confusing, or created a sense of pressure and or manipulation in the way it was expressed.

> Once people begin to flow in the gifts of the Holy Spirit, they also need to learn some principles for how to function appropriately in those gifts.

This was the problem in the Corinthian church. The apostle Paul, when writing 1 Corinthians, was addressing some of the internal struggles the church in Corinth was experiencing. One of the problems was the misuse and abuse of the supernatural gifts and experiences of the Holy Spirit.

What was going on? Their services were a spiritual circus. If you had entered the weekly services at the church in Corinth you would have seen nothing but confusion. Some people were interrupting the service by standing up and randomly speaking in tongues. Others were trying to take over the service by speaking out words of prophecy for lengthy periods of time. One person would be speaking publicly, and then another person would try to talk over them, and there would be a "war for airtime," so to speak.

People were leaving services frustrated, confused, and wondering what it was all about. What was most concerning about this environment was the impact it was having on the Corinthian church's ability to reach people who needed Christ. Paul expressed it like this,

"If the whole church comes together and everyone speaks in tongues, and inquirers or unbelievers come in, will they not say that you are out of your mind" (1 Corinthians 14:23)?

This may be the unspoken danger you feel as you read this book. You might be thinking, *I'm with you. I believe the power of God is needed as a witness to the resurrection. I believe the Holy Spirit is needed in the life of every believer. I believe that speaking in tongues is an experience for today. But I'm afraid that if I start to live this or lead people in this, our church is going to become a crazy charismatic environment that is awkward, confusing, and limited in its ability to reach out to those who are lost."*

How do I make this work in my life and not become part of a spiritual crazy house? The instructions that we find in 1 Corinthians 14 provide the pathway to proper function and use. Now, the content of this chapter is less about the baptism in the Holy Spirit and more about the down-the-line impact of the baptism in the Holy Spirit. Once you are baptized in the Holy Spirit, you will begin to function in the gifts of the Holy Spirit as well.

Once people begin to flow in the gifts of the Holy Spirit, they also need to learn some principles for how to function appropriately in those gifts. This is what Paul carefully outlined in 1 Corinthians 14. You may want to put this book down for a moment, find that chapter in the Bible, and read it. Then come back and read through the various principles in the following pages.

PRINCIPLE 1: EXPECTATION

"Follow the way of love and eagerly desire the gifts of the Spirit"
(1 Corinthians 14:1).

In the first verse of this chapter, Paul mentions two things that must be kept in balance. Some want to (1) follow the way of love. They want to make sure that everything is done with others in mind. They want to design church services people can relate to and understand.

They want their spiritual experiences to draw people to Jesus not turn them away. They want to make the Bible and the gospel relevant to those who are far from God.

Others want to (2) eagerly desire the gifts of the Spirit. They want to see every aspect of God's power released in their lives. If there's a spiritual experience to be had, they want to experience it. They want every drop of the Holy Spirit to be manifested in their lives. They want to design church services where people have the liberty and freedom to soak in the presence of God and experience the transformative power of the Holy Spirit.

Too many times, we're on one side or the other of this equation. Paul teaches that we need to have both to function biblically. It isn't enough to love people; we also need to "eagerly desire spiritual gifts." It isn't enough to want to flow in the powerful gifts of the Spirit and not be aware of the need to love and reach out to people. Both must be kept in balance. Both must be our passionate pursuit.

So which one do you currently lean toward? How can you make sure you are intentionally pursuing both? Are you focused on loving people? Are you eagerly and intentionally expecting to be used in the supernatural?

PRINCIPLE 2: EDIFICATION

"For anyone who speaks in a tongue does not speak to people but to God. Indeed, no one understands them; they utter mysteries by the Spirit. But the one who prophesies speaks to people for their strengthening, encouraging and comfort"
(1 Corinthians 12:2–3).

Whenever God works supernaturally through the life of one person to meet the need of another, it is always for the purpose of edification. What does it mean to edify? The verses define it: to strengthen, encourage, and comfort. Some have said it like this: to

> When we are with others, we have to aim our experiences with the Holy Spirit toward the edification of everyone present in the room.

build up, to cheer up, and to lift up.

This is the standard and motivation for being used in the power of God. My hunger to be used by God and to experience the power of the Holy Spirit is not just for me. Yes, God wants to heal me, to restore me, to empower me, to use me. Yes, God wants to use my lips to pray supernatural prayers. It's amazing to experience the presence of God Himself in our lives.

But when we are with others, we have to aim our experiences with the Holy Spirit toward the edification of everyone present in the room. When I pray in private, I can feel free to speak in tongues, sing, or shout for joy to go deeper into God's presence. But when I'm with others (especially those who are not yet believers), I need to consider how my actions and responses to the Holy Spirit are affecting them.

PRINCIPLE 3: NORMALIZATION

"Again, if the trumpet does not sound a clear call, who will get ready for battle? So it is with you. Unless you speak intelligible words with your tongue, how will anyone know what you are saying? You will just be speaking into the air. Undoubtedly there are all sorts of languages in the world, yet none of them is without meaning. If then I do not grasp the meaning of what someone is saying, I am a foreigner to the speaker, and the speaker is a foreigner to me. So it is with you. Since you are eager for gifts of the Spirit, try to excel in those that build up the church"
(1 Corinthians 14:8–12).

This may be the biggest issue of all when it comes to functioning appropriately with spiritual gifts. Whatever we say or do has to be expressed in such a way that it can be understood and received by those who hear us. Remember, the goal is to build up those who are present. So we need to fashion what we say and do so others can understand it and apply it.

I grew up in a Pentecostal church and experienced many services that were a lot like the "spiritual circus" in the church at Corinth. What was typical in a lot of these events was this: Whoever was being used in a spiritual gift would suddenly become a different person. Their voice would tremble, the volume would rise. It was startling, emotional, and sometimes a bit scary.

What I believed about the supernatural was this: When God used someone it was like a lightning bolt hit them. They would lose control of who they were. God would take over and make them do and say things that were beyond understanding. It was like detonating a powerful spiritual explosive device in a meeting that would spray all kinds of spiritual debris everywhere.

Often I didn't understand how what happened benefited anyone in the room, but I didn't want to argue with what the Holy Spirit was doing. So I endured it and ignored it. I wasn't against it. But honestly, I wasn't really interested in having this experience that seemed so odd and out of place to me. The way in which spiritual gifts were used in my experience did several things to me:

- I believed that functioning in the supernatural was only for a special class of people who were eerily in touch with God in a way that I was not.
- I was inoculated against wanting to be used in spiritual gifts because I was unwilling to become so emotional and demonstrative in front of others.
- I began to believe that spiritual gifts could only happen in Pentecostal worship services. I never heard stories of them functioning outside of a church building.

- I was hesitant to bring my friends to church with me because I didn't know how to explain to them the weird emotional explosions that might happen during the service.

I have since learned that functioning in spiritual gifts doesn't have to be spooky, emotional, or spoken in old King James English. In fact, what I see written in 1 Corinthians 14 is that the explosive way these gifts are so often practiced is potentially a hindrance to their proper use.

What I teach people now is that spiritual gifts should be used in a normal tone of voice, and out of your authentic personality. When God starts to move through you, you may feel emotions well up within you, but you are capable of managing your emotions in order to convey a message or word of encouragement in the most effective way for the people who are listening.

Spiritual gifts aren't released when a lightning bolt strikes you; spiritual gifts are released when you decide to partner with the inner prompting of the Holy Spirit to speak out and believe for God to work in the life of another person. We should expect that God will release the gifts of the Holy Spirit through us during a worship service. But even more than that, we should expect that God will release the gifts of the Holy Spirit in our everyday lives, Monday through Friday as well.

We should practice using the gifts in a normal way. What I like to teach is this: If you were in a grocery store and God spoke to you about someone you saw in one of the aisles, how would you use that gift? Hopefully you wouldn't close your eyes, shake, lift your voice, and start to say, "Thus says the Lord . . ."

Wouldn't that totally freak people out?

Rather, you might approach that person in a humble tone. Introduce yourself. Explain what happened to you as you walked down the aisle. Explain how the Holy Spirit prompted you to say something. Present your message in a sensitive way, aware of your surroundings and in touch with the person's reactions and response.

This is the way the Holy Spirit wants to work.

PRINCIPLE 4: EXPLANATION

*"Now, brothers and sisters, if I come to you and speak
in tongues, what good will I be to you, unless I bring you some
revelation or knowledge or prophecy or word of instruction? Even
in the case of lifeless things that make sounds, such as the pipe or
harp, how will anyone know what tune is being played unless
there is a distinction in the notes"
(1 Corinthians 14:6–7)?*

I have found that most people are completely open to the supernatural, especially if the atmosphere they are in feels safe. People don't feel safe when they don't understand what is happening around them, especially if all of a sudden someone gets really emotional and does something unusual or unique right beside them or right in front of them.

Now, I realize that safety isn't our only goal. We want power. We want transformation. We want to see people healed, and restored, and visited by the presence of God. But I believe we can do all of that, and at the same time make people feel safe enough that they can relax and remain open to what God is doing.

The key to feeling safe is having someone there to interpret what is going on. If we slow the process down enough to say, "This is what is happening; this is what the Bible teaches; and this is why this is important," then we gain the trust of those we are trying to reach.

PRINCIPLE 5: INCLUSION

*"The spirits of prophets are subject to the control of prophets.
For God is not a God of disorder but of peace—as in all
the congregations of the Lord's people"
(1 Corinthians 14:32–33).*

> I have found that most people are completely open to the supernatural, especially if the atmosphere they are in feels safe.

When I teach this, I get some pushback from people who come from traditional Pentecostal backgrounds. They say, "When the Holy Spirit comes on me, I can't control how the message comes out. In fact, if I try to control it, I limit what the Holy Spirit wants to do."

My response is always to go back to the Bible. Paul teaches in this I Corinthians passage that those who are prophets (meaning they are speaking under the inspiration of the Holy Spirit) can control the function of their own spirits. As they hear from God, they can manage the way that message is delivered. "For God is not a God of disorder but of peace."

I have titled this principle Inclusion for a reason. For over 100 years, Pentecostal churches have practiced the use of spiritual gifts in worship services by an interruption in the service. From the days of the Azuza Street Mission—when people gathered for worship on the top floor of an old hall with sawdust floors, wooden benches, and no electronic sound systems— the practice has been for a person to stand up in the service, take the floor, and declare a word from God. Sometimes, one person interrupts the service by speaking in tongues. Then another person interrupts the service by interpreting those tongues. This has been the normal function in Pentecostal churches for years.

After pastoring at Allison Park Church for over a decade, I realized that this interruptive style, perhaps more than anything else, was what made people feel unsafe. They never knew who would speak, from where in the auditorium, what they would say, or even whether or not the speaker was credible and trustworthy. Many times people couldn't hear the speaker or couldn't understand the message because the speaker wasn't speaking into a microphone. It was messy and confusing.

That's when I realized: The world has changed since 1906.

No one ever stands in the back of any room and shouts out a message. That may have been the culture of the day before sound systems, stages, etc. Town hall meetings and small country venues were the order of the day, but not anymore. That's why an interruption in the service with someone shouting out a message from God seems so unusual and unsettling in our current culture.

So we changed how we function with spiritual gifts in our worship services. When someone feels they have a word or prophecy, instead of shouting from their seats, they simply come to one of our pastoral team members and share with them what they are sensing. Then, we either have them come up onto the platform to share or we convey the message to the congregation on their behalf.

This one change has done more to make everyone feel safe than anything else when it comes to our function. And this one change led to several other things:

- Quiet and shy people who would never have shouted from the back are being used in spiritual gifts.
- People who attend our church feel safe and are bringing their friends to church in greater numbers.
- We are teaching how to use the gifts in a normal tone and an explained fashion.
- More and more people are using spiritual gifts in their everyday lives.

PRINCIPLE 6: DEMONSTRATION

And you should imitate me, just as I imitate Christ
(1 Corinthians 11:1).

Most of this chapter is spent on bringing balance to areas of practice where there is excess. But I want to emphasize that there can be no *balance* without a *beginning*. There's no need for parameters when nothing is practiced. Perhaps you have heard it stated, "Better to have wild fire, than no fire at all."

When it comes to actual fire, I'm not sure that is a truism! But when it comes to the working of the Holy Spirit, I believe it is absolutely true. It's possible to take so many precautions to avoid offending or scaring people that we totally eliminate any opportunity for God to operate in our midst. It's actually impossible to model for people something that we don't practice or pursue ourselves.

One of the things I so appreciated about my parents was that they had a faith that was more than just words. I'll never forget the day my dad came home from visiting the hospital. One of the members of our church had become ill and wasn't expected to live through the night. My father was called to the bedside to comfort the family as they watched their father die.

Standing beside the hospital bed, my dad reminded the family, "Doctors provide a prognosis, but God has the final word. We can still believe God for a miracle." As they prayed, the Holy Spirit moved and Mr. Thurston not only survived the night, he walked out of the hospital the next day—totally healed. This moment impressed me as a teenager more than I can express. Amazing thoughts swirled through my head: *God must truly be real! My dad knows God and knows how to pray! Following Jesus isn't boring; it's an adventure!*

I'm the father of five kids (and now the grandfather of my first grandchild). My desire is to demonstrate to them a faith that has more than just principles and values. I want to give them a faith that carries transformational power. As a pastor, I want to introduce my people to more than just good teaching, descriptions of stories from long ago, and encouraging thoughts for their lives. My desire is to introduce them to the *person* of the Holy Spirit and to demonstrate before them a life that is lived out of Holy Spirit power.

PRINCIPLE 7: PREPARATION

What then shall we say, brothers and sisters? When you come
together, each of you has a hymn, or a word of instruction,
a revelation, a tongue or an interpretation. Everything must
be done so that the church may be built up
(1 Corinthians 14:26).

Because the Holy Spirit lives within every believer, and since He is never without the capacity to demonstrate His power, we should anticipate that He will constantly show up in our lives. It's an everyday expectation; a moment by moment anticipation. Every time we attend a church service or a small group or encounter someone in need, we are living moments filled with divine potential because the Holy Spirit fills our lives.

Bruce Wilkinson has written one of the best books I have ever read about this kind of preparation to live a supernatural life. The book is titled, *You Were Born for This: Seven Keys for Predictable Miracles.* He paints this picture for us, "You were born to be a living link between heaven and earth. You were born to be God's ambassador in the Everyday Miracle Territory, making Him visible in unforgettable ways. The miraculous touches of heaven that God wants to accomplish His will come in all sizes, but mostly they'll be of the personal everyday sort that you can be a part of. Why? Because God passionately desires to show Himself strong for you and through you, and because every person you meet has a significant need that only God can meet."[7]

You are God's "miracle delivery system" is the phrase Bruce coins in this book. I love that picture of what we are. You are a carrier of the Holy Spirit. He is ready to move in your life and in the lives of those around you at any given moment. Therefore, we should live tuned up, prayed up, and ready to be used by God!

DISCUSSION QUESTIONS FOR CHAPTER SEVEN

1. What is the worst customer service experience you have ever had? What made it so bad?

2. In your opinion, are most churches aware of what outsiders feel? Are we, as the church, good at creating environments where people feel welcome and safe?

3. How do you make people feel comfortable when they enter your home?

4. What kinds of things are necessary for you to do, if God wanted you to minister to someone who was brand new to God or to church?

5. What will happen to the church if it ever stops creating room for the Holy Spirit to move in our environments? What's the balance?

6. Have you ever seen this done really well? Where someone ministered to you in a powerful Holy Spirit way, and yet maintained humility and sensitivity? Describe this moment and why it so impacted you.

CHAPTER EIGHT

IT'S TRANSFORMATIONAL!

Sometimes it seems safer to have just enough God to get to heaven, but not so much that he radically alters our lives.[8]

—CHRIS HODGES

One of the most heartbreaking things I have done as a pastor is to walk with someone through a painful divorce or the breakdown of what had been a seemingly vibrant relationship. One instance, in particular, stands out to me as perhaps the most shocking and agonizing heartbreak I have ever seen.

I was in the room when my friend received the news. Not only was his wife cheating on him, she was cheating on him with his best friend! After the initial shock, questions flooded his mind. *How long has this been going on? When did it start? How did it start? Why? How could you? What do I do now? How do I even begin to function again?*

No physical earthquake could have rocked his world more. It was a life-altering moment, without question. The only choice he had was whether to let this painful disappointment alter his life in a way that would destroy him or let it lead him to a place that would make him a better man.

Now, I know that seems like an extreme oversimplification. Even as I wrote that last sentence, I realized how insensitive it sounds. After all, he did nothing to deserve what happened to him. He wasn't a bad guy or a poor husband. The destructiveness of that moment had little to do with his choices. It had to do with the choices of those around him, those closest to him, mind you! So how could his decision have anything to do with the destructive potential of that situation?

Please understand, I'm not saying that his choices could have prevented the damage done by others. The pain of that moment was 100 percent a result of the acts of others. But the trajectory of his life from that moment forward was very much dependent on the choices he made about how he would respond to it.

Charles Swindoll is famous for saying, "Life is 10 percent what happens to you and 90 percent how you respond to it." I watched as my friend responded like a champion. Actually, he made three decisions that truly saved and changed his life.

1. He immersed himself in the Bible. Every time he faced a painful memory, or the image of his best friend and his wife together, he redirected his thoughts toward memorizing the Word of God. He told me, "That's the only thing that kept me from going crazy."

2. He became an active participant in a men's small group. These guys became his armor bearers and stood with him in the lowest moments of his life.

3. He filled his life with worship. His job involved driving a truck, so he had a lot of free thought moments during the day. When he wasn't memorizing Scripture, he spent hours in worship: music blaring away in the cab of the truck with him singing at the top of his lungs. And since he was baptized in the Holy Spirit, he would also pray in the Spirit throughout the day.

What I can tell you is this. Not only did he make it through the worst trial of his entire life, he came through on the other side of it whole and powerful. Prior to this tragedy he was a tepid or lukewarm believer. He attended church. He served on occasion. But his walk with God was shallow.

Something happened to him when the pain of the moment drove

him into a place of desperation. As he practiced daily disciplines of partnership with God, he became incredibly mature and strong. Honestly, his walk with God challenged me. Every time I was around him, I was affected by his spirit.

And somehow, after all of this, God gave him the grace to forgive his wife. She repented. She worked like crazy to earn back his trust. She joined him in his desperate pursuit of the presence and promises of God, and over time, the wound healed and their marriage was restored. Two decades later, I can tell you they are still married and actively serving God together. Their three kids have been raised in a home that could have been broken for good but has now stood the test of time.

Several chapters ago I mentioned the Greek word that Jesus used to describe the Holy Spirit. "And I will ask the Father, and he will give you another advocate to help you and be with you forever—the Spirit of truth" (John 14:16-17). The phrase "another advocate" is that Greek word *paraclete*. A paraclete is someone who lives within us to impart to us resources that we don't have on our own. Like a parasite lives within us to rob us of our strength, a paraclete lives within us to impart to us His strength.

Jesus used another example to describe this close relationship, "I am the vine; you are the branches. If you remain in me and I in you, you will bear much fruit; apart from me you can do nothing" (John 15:5). The imagery is clear. Life flows through the vine, like sap through the trunk of a tree. As long as the branch is connected to the vine, it's connected to the source and flow of life. When it's disconnected, it dies.

A connected branch has capacity. It remains strong. It flourishes. It produces leaves and fruit in abundance. A connected branch has life that isn't self-produced; it comes from another source, the vine. A disconnected branch is not only dead, it is unproductive. "Apart from me," Jesus declared, "you can do nothing."

Connected to the vine, I can do anything. Disconnected from the vine, I can do nothing!

So here's the application. When I choose to surrender my life to Jesus Christ, and I put my faith in who He is, I become connected to "the vine." It's like being grafted into the trunk of the vine because previously we were "dead in our transgressions and sins" (Ephesians 2:1) but now God made us alive in Christ (Ephesians 2:5–6).

As soon as our dead branch connects to the vine, the Holy Spirit ignites something inside of us. Not only are we saved from the consequences of our sin and forgiven and made righteous in the sight of God, we are regenerated or infused with life on the inside. Jesus said in John 3 that we are "born again" or "born of the Spirit."

> Connected to the vine, I can do anything. Disconnected from the vine, I can do nothing!

A new reality has come into effect in our lives. We now have a reservoir of life to draw from within our own being, and since the Holy Spirit is such a dynamic person, He adds to us everything we need for any situation we face. Whenever we have a lack, we can look to the Holy Spirit because He is and He has all that we need.

HE SHARES HIS DISPOSITION

If we stick with this metaphor of the vine and branches, we see another example of the outcome of this relationship. The apostle Paul tells us the kind of fruit we can expect in our lives as a result of this connection: "The fruit of the Spirit is love, joy, peace, forbearance, kindness, goodness, faithfulness, gentleness and self-control" (Galatians 5:22–23).

Here's the fantastic news! The Holy Spirit provides everything we need for every situation.

- When I'm weary, tired, discouraged, and ready to give up, I have no joy on the inside. However, the Holy Spirit never lacks joy; it's always His disposition. Since He lives inside of me, He's willing to share His joy with me. All I have to do is tap into His presence.
- If you're a single parent raising kids on your own, working two jobs, and you have run out of patience with all the challenges you face, the Holy Spirit is perfectly patient. When you choose to worship or pray in the Spirit, He will release more than enough patience into your soul.
- When you're anxious and tied up in knots over a situation, the Holy Spirit never has anxiety. He only knows peace. He has more than enough peace to share.

"Do not be anxious about anything, but in every situation, by prayer and petition, with thanksgiving, present your requests to God. And the peace of God, which transcends all understanding, will guard your hearts and your minds in Christ Jesus" (Philippians 4:6–7). The peace of God is given to us not as a quality that is independent of the Holy Spirit's work in our lives. It is given to us as a quality of soul that is deposited within us because of His work in our lives. So when you take time every day to pray, you aren't only practicing an excellent spiritual discipline but you're activating the Holy Spirit's work in your life and intentionally accessing His disposition (the fruits of the Spirit).

HE SHARES HIS CAPACITY

Here's a second piece of fantastic news. Not only does the Holy Spirit have an amazing and unshakable disposition, He also has precise and powerful solutions for every problem we could ever face. We typically call these solutions the gifts of the Spirit. Notice this description:

> Now to each one the manifestation of the Spirit is given for the common good. To one there is given through the Spirit a message of wisdom, to another a message of knowledge by means of the same Spirit, to another faith by the same Spirit, to another gifts of healing by that one Spirit, to another miraculous powers, to another prophecy, to another distinguishing between spirits, to another speaking in different kinds of tongues, and to still another the interpretation of tongues. All these are the work of one and the same Spirit, and he distributes them to each one, just as he determines. (1 Corinthians 12:7–11)

Notice a few things that are taught here:

- The Spirit gives these gifts for the common good (everyone's benefit).
- Since the Spirit gives these gifts we know that the Spirit possesses these gifts.
- All of these supernatural solutions are the work of the same Spirit.
- The Spirit gives these gifts to each of us as we need or as He determines.

So here's the conclusion: The Holy Spirit has all the power we need, all the timely information we need, and all of the solutions we need for any and all situations we face. He is willing to share that power, information, and solutions with us at the moment we need it. Because we have the Holy Spirit—or because He has us—we can expect Him to explode on the scene with His provision at just the right time.

I'm not sure who taught me this definition for the gifts of the Spirit, but I like it: "The gifts of the Spirit are divine explosions of God's power through the life of a surrendered believer to meet human

> The potential for an outbreak of God's power resides in you every day, every moment, in every place, no matter the situation.

need at precisely the time it is needed."

Every day we walk around with the third person of the Trinity alive within our souls. The same Spirit who raised Jesus from the dead gives life to our mortal bodies (Romans 8:11). This means that the potential for an outbreak of God's power resides in you every day, every moment, in every place, no matter the situation.

Can you imagine what a tragedy it is that so many Holy Spirit-empowered believers simply choose to live out of their own strength and solutions rather than out of His? What a shame that we don't realize and access the capacity He wants to make available to us! Too many of us live as if there were no Holy Spirit at all. We live as if He's a last resort for help when a crisis becomes more than we can handle.

Every day we have the potential to access His precise and powerful solutions to our problems if we tune in to His operation within our lives. This is critical, not only for us to live overcoming and godly lives but for the world around us to receive ministry from God through us. You and I walk around every day with the potential to change the world, to see miracles released, and to have signs and wonders manifest to prove that Jesus is alive.

What that requires is a daily approach to activating the Holy Spirit's work as we worship, pray, and live.

HE SHARES HIS UNDERSTANDING

The final piece of fantastic news I want to mention here is that the Holy Spirit always has complete understanding and incredible insight into whatever I need to know. Jesus encouraged His disciples with this on the final night before His crucifixion. He had let them know He was going to leave them and how much better it would be for them after He sent them the Holy Spirit.

> All this I have spoken while still with you. But the Advocate, the Holy Spirit, whom the Father will send in my name, will teach you all things and will remind you of everything I have said to you. Peace I leave with you; my peace I give you. I do not give to you as the world gives. Do not let your hearts be troubled and do not be afraid. (John 14:25–27)

The Holy Spirit will teach you *all* things and will remind you of *everything*. When I'm confused and don't know what to do, the Holy Spirit knows. When I face a situation that is more complicated than I can figure out, it isn't complicated to Him. When I need to understand who God is or what the Bible is teaching in a difficult passage, the Holy Spirit is there to give the insight I need. When I'm in an argument with my wife and I can't seem to figure out what to do or say, the Holy Spirit has perfect understanding of who Melodie is, what she needs, and how I need to respond to her.

The Holy Spirit knows everything! And He's willing to share what He knows with me.

A few years ago, I decided to preach a series of sermons about the Holy Spirit. It was a Friday night, and I had prepared my message for the weekend. My goal was to communicate the concept I just outlined: that the Holy Spirit has perfect understanding and wants to share it with us in our moments of need.

As I was falling asleep, I was praying about my message and meditating on the truth of the statements Jesus made in John 14. In the middle of the night, I woke up with an overwhelming sense of the presence of God. Actually, I woke myself up praying in tongues. Now, I know that last statement makes me look incredibly spiritual, so let me clarify that this has only happened two or three times in my entire life. Most of the time, when I wake up in the middle of the night I'm thinking about pizza or dreaming some crazy dream about a movie I watched the night before. But on this occasion, I woke up hearing myself speaking in tongues. And as I awoke, I felt the inner whisper of the Holy Spirit say something very specific to me: *When you speak to your people this weekend, tell them I am so much smarter than they are.*

When I felt this prompting, I laughed out loud. Then I heard Him speak to me again: *Tell them I'm so much smarter than they are and I want them to know that.* So I thought about the logic of this statement. At first, it sounded almost arrogant. But it wasn't arrogance; it was just a statement of fact. He *is* so much smarter than we are!

> "For my thoughts are not your thoughts, neither are your ways my ways," declares the LORD." As the heavens are higher than the earth, so are my ways higher than your ways and my thoughts than your thoughts." (Isaiah 55:8-9)

The next day, when I spoke to my church I told them what the Holy Spirit had directed me to say. "The Holy Spirit wants you to know that He is so much smarter than you are, and He wants to share with you what He knows. Too often you're depending on your own thoughts to solve unsolvable problems. But the Holy Spirit is much smarter than you. He isn't just a little smarter than you. It's actually not even close. You aren't even in the same ballpark when it comes to what He knows. So stop depending on your own thoughts, and ask for His help."

When I declared this, there was a breakthrough in the atmosphere. We all laughed out loud together at this obvious truth and then we began to worship. We asked the Holy Spirit to help us with our problems. The pressure lifted. The stress disappeared. Life and peace began to flow, because He is so much smarter than we are and when we trust Him we can access all we need for the moment we are in.

IT'S ABOUT LIVING OUT OF A DIFFERENT SOURCE

This understanding about who the Holy Spirit is and how He works in my life to lead me, empower me, and transform me, has changed my approach to life. I no longer approach my daily devotional time just from a place of spiritual disciplines. Yes, I realize that spiritual disciplines like prayer, Bible reading, and fasting are critical to spiritual formation. Growth happens as I learn to discipline myself in my relationship with God. This duty to pursue God is important, but it's so much more than just a duty and so much more than just discipline.

If I approach my daily time with God as an encounter with a *Person*, then my expectations are much different. My devotional life isn't something I do for God, a set of prayers I pray, and lists of Bible verses I read. My devotional life is activating the operation of the Holy Spirit in my life.

- I don't just read the Bible, I read the Bible with Him for His insight and illumination.
- I don't just pray, I pray with Him. Actually, as I pray in the Spirit, I let Him pray through me with precision according to the will of God.
- When I finish that season of devotions, I know I enter my day ready to live out of His disposition, prepared to deliver His solutions to a needy world, and aware that He is so much smarter than I am in every situation I face.

DISCUSSION QUESTIONS FOR CHAPTER EIGHT

1. Describe a moment in your life when your cell phone ran out of power at just the wrong time.
2. Read John 15:1–7. What are your observations from these verses about the power source for your spiritual life? List at least three things from these verses.
3. Read Galatians 5:22–23. How does it make you feel to know that the Holy Spirit always has these qualities in His possession?
4. What practical steps are involved in accessing the disposition and capacity of the Holy Spirit in these areas of life?
5. We all have to choose whether to live out of our own strength and spirit or to live out of the strength of the Holy Spirit. The choice is an obvious one, but why is this so difficult for us to practice?
6. What will you do this week to live out of God's Holy Spirit?

CHAPTER NINE
IT'S MISSIONAL!

We are the product of our past but we don't have to be prisoners of it.[9]

—RICK WARREN

H e was twenty-three years old when it happened. After a night
of heavy drinking and partying, Justin Maslanka was driving
home. Not only was he driving while drunk, he was moving at a very
high rate of speed. The car careened out of control, bounced across
the road, and came to a halt when it hit a large tree.

To say the car was totaled is an understatement. The bumper was
mangled, the entire frame twisted, and every window shattered. But
somehow, Justin survived the crash. The car bent in a shape that
allowed just enough space for his head and body to survive. It was a
miracle and he knew it.

While recovering from his injuries, Justin's mom provided the
needed statement to accompany this dose of reality. "God saved
your life, Justin! You should be dead right now. I have been praying
for you all along, and I believe that God has spared you for a purpose.
It's time you get right with God."

It's not that Justin didn't know the truth about Jesus. He had been
to church. He attended the youth ministry at Allison Park Church
off and on. He believed there is a God. He understood who Jesus
is and that He died on the cross for us. He had no issue with the
concept of God or His purpose for us. He just didn't feel the need to
surrender his life to Jesus. "Maybe later when I'm older and I've had
my fun, then I'll surrender my life to God."

But after that near-death experience, Justin was ready to get his life right with God. The very next day he gave his life to Jesus Christ. He started to attend Allison Park Church on a regular basis, but knew that he needed to do more, so he got involved in the youth ministry. This gave him an opportunity to be mentored by Cullen Allen, who was serving as the youth pastor at the time.

> These disciples had seen and heard something that had the capacity to change the world!

Cullen told Justin about the baptism in the Holy Spirit. He sat down with him and explained what Jesus had explained to His disciples, "You will receive power when the Holy Spirit comes upon you; and you will be my witnesses in Jerusalem, and in all Judea and Samaria, and to the ends of the earth" (Acts 1:8). Cullen explained that the Holy Spirit came to give us *power* for life, "It's not that we get the Holy Spirit at the moment we are baptized in the Holy Spirit; we get the Holy Spirit when we get saved. When we are baptized in the Holy Spirit, the Holy Spirit gets us!"

So Cullen prayed for Justin to be baptized in the Holy Spirit. The Spirit of God came upon Justin in a powerful way. Not only could he sense the presence of God, but Justin began to pray out in tongues. It was like an explosion of praise came out of his lips as he threw his head back and was swept away in the flow of God's power.

I saw Justin just a few days after this experience. "Pastor Jeff," he said excitedly, "you won't believe what has happened to me! On Tuesday, I was baptized in the Holy Spirit, and since then, I have already led two people to Christ. Today, I was just hanging out at Borders Bookstore, getting a cup of coffee, and all of the sudden I felt this urging on the inside that I needed to go over and tell this guy sitting at the table next to me about Jesus. So I told him my story, about how God saved my life in the car crash, and I told him how I surrendered my life to Jesus. He said that was what he needed to do as well. So I prayed for him right there in Borders!"

Can you see this change?

One moment, Justin was partying, drinking, and running from God. Then God intervened and protected him from death in a horrific collision. So Justin surrendered his life to Jesus, which was what he needed to do to become right with God. He started living for God. He wanted God to use him. Then after he was baptized in the Holy Spirit, Justin stepped into a dimension of purpose that energized his every moment. He knew he was alive for a purpose, and his purpose was to lead people to be saved through Jesus Christ, in the same way that Jesus had saved him.

Today, Justin Maslanka serves as the pastor of the CityReach Church in Cleveland, Ohio. His church has a Men's Hope Home and is being used powerfully to help addicts and alcoholics get free from life-controlling substances and find hope in a relationship with Christ. Justin is a powerful preacher and is being used all over northern Ohio to lead people to Christ. He would tell you that this capacity to win people to Christ started with the experience the Bible calls the baptism in the Holy Spirit.

Let's examine what Jesus promised:

> "You will receive power when the Holy Spirit comes upon you and you will be my witnesses in Jerusalem, and in all Judea and Samaria, and to the ends of the earth." (Acts 1:8)

Remember that Jesus had given His disciples the Great Commission to go into all the world and make disciples of everyone everywhere and teach them to obey the way that Jesus had taught them to live. This was the purpose given to the disciples at that moment, and it is still His purpose for every one of His followers today. So He instructed His disciples to wait in Jerusalem for the *gift* that His Father promised (Acts 1:4).

THE GIFT THAT BRINGS POWER

Jesus said that the gift He was giving, being baptized in the Holy Spirit, would bring power. The word in the Greek that Jesus used is the word *dunamis,* which is a root word from which we get the word "dynamite." It implies an explosive release of power that proves the testimony of those witnessing to the resurrection.

> "You will receive *power* when the Holy Spirit comes upon you and you will be my *witnesses.*" (Acts 1:8, emphasis added)

Sometimes we forget the context of these statements. What were the disciples to be witnesses about? What had they seen and heard? If someone put them on the stand in a courtroom, what would they testify that they had experienced? These disciples had seen and heard something that had the capacity to change the world!

They had been witnesses to the resurrection of Jesus!

Yes, they had walked with Him during three years of ministry on earth. Yes, they had watched Him put on trial, be falsely accused, beaten, and crucified. But what was extremely remarkable was the fact that they had seen Jesus alive *after* He was in the grave for three days! "After his suffering, he [Jesus] presented himself to them and gave many convincing proofs that He was alive" (Acts 1:3).

Jesus is alive! He wants to prove it to the world! He is looking for people who will represent Him on earth and work with Him to prove it to those who need someone to testify to them about His resurrection and His ongoing activity on earth today. So the Holy Spirit was imparted to the disciples to give them power to prove the resurrection.

Simon Peter provided proof of the resurrection in Acts 3. He released physical healing to a crippled beggar at the Temple and the man began walking and jumping and declaring the healing power of a risen Jesus.

"Fellow Israelites," Peter said, "why does this surprise you? Why do you stare at us as if by our own power or godliness we had made this man walk. The God of Abraham, Isaac and Jacob, the God of our fathers, has glorified his servant Jesus. You handed him over to be killed. . . . You killed the author of life, but God raised Him from the dead. We are witnesses of this" (Acts 3:12–15).

The baptism in the Holy Spirit allowed Peter to step into the power of God in such a way as to see miracles released in the world. The baptism in the Holy Spirit was the gateway to the supernatural in Peter's life, and it can be the gateway to the supernatural release of God's power in your life.

In 2006, I had the opportunity to be part of a huge outreach (we call them festivals) in Harar, Ethiopia. Harar is one of the holiest cities in all Islam: it's population is 98 percent Muslim. We went to declare to the people of Harar that Jesus is the Son of God. We went to share the love of God with these Muslims and to offer them proof that Jesus is risen from the dead.

But you can't really prove the resurrection with just words.

There was a man in the city of Harar who was born both deaf and mute. He was forty-two years old. He was well known in the city because he pumped gas at one of the local gas stations in a prominent place in the city. This man attended the second night of the outdoor Festival. One of our team prayed over him in the name of Jesus and as he was prayed for, Jesus demonstrated Himself to that city. The man's ears opened up and he could hear. We brought him up onto the stage, and asked him to prove his healing by repeating what he heard. Into the microphone, this man did his best to repeat the syllables that he was now hearing for the very first time.

As you can imagine, this was an incredibly impressive moment. The crowd began to whisper to one another in disbelief, and then they began to laugh, and shout, and dance. Muslims were dancing in the streets at the healing of a deaf man who was cured by being prayed over in the *name of Jesus!* The next night, 17,000 Muslims stood in the field to hear the message of the risen Jesus. Thousands of them prayed to give their lives to Christ.

THE GIFT THAT BRINGS PASSION

"You will receive power when the Holy Spirit comes on you; and you will be my witnesses in Jerusalem, and in all Judea and Samaria, and to the ends of the earth" (Act 1:8).

As soon as Justin Maslanka received the baptism in the Holy Spirit, he had a burden and desire to tell people about Jesus. He carried a burning sensation in his chest. The Holy Spirit was activated within him, and he saw people through the passion of a loving God who wants everyone to be rescued. No one had to tell Justin to share his story with people. The Holy Spirit prompted Justin everywhere he went. No one had to build a program for Justin to share his story; Justin felt compelled to do that everywhere he went.

After I was baptized in the Holy Spirit, I also had an undeniable passion to see my friends come to know Jesus. I was a sophomore in a public high school and had many good friends who didn't have a relationship with Jesus. Every day on my way to school, I felt a burning inside of me compelling me to do something to reach my friends at school. So a few of us students got together and started a prayer meeting before the homeroom bell rang to start the day. Slowly, that early morning prayer meeting grew until there were eighty students standing in a circle and praying together in the name of Jesus.

When you're baptized in the Holy Spirit, you'll become part of God's strategic plan to reach the world with the hope of Jesus Christ. The words of Jesus in Acts 1:8 are strategic. They were to start in Jerusalem, the place where they all lived. It was their hometown, their culture, their comfort zone. But they weren't to stop there. Jesus instructed them to go beyond their comfort zone into all of Judea and Samaria, different locations with different racial groups and cultures. He wanted them to love beyond their comfort zone and to reach past themselves into places they would never have chosen to go on their own.

As we know, many of these disciples didn't stop with Samaria. They traveled to Europe, India, Africa, China, and beyond. They

> When you're baptized in the Holy Spirit, you'll become part of God's strategic plan to reach the world with the hope of Jesus Christ.

were driven by a sense of passion for something beyond themselves. No longer were they simply surviving or living boring, passionless lives. They were set on fire to do something with their lives that would last for all eternity.

THE GIFT THAT BRINGS PRODUCTIVITY

The 120 people who gathered in the upper room on the Day of Pentecost when the Holy Spirit was first poured out went on to change the world! Think about it, 120 people. Jesus had ministered for three years and had done countless miracles. He had appeared in resurrected form to over 500 people. But only 120 were present in the upper room. Have you ever wondered where all the others were? Three hundred and eighty people saw Jesus after the resurrection, physically alive, and they weren't present to wait for the baptism in the Holy Spirit.

Where were the 5,000 who were fed the loaves and the fishes? Where were the multitudes who had cheered Jesus on Palm Sunday? Where were all those who had been healed or touched in some way? There were only 120 people in the upper room, but after being baptized in the Holy Spirit, those 120 were so empowered they started a revolution that has changed the history of the world.

Today there are two billion people who call themselves Christians. Millions upon millions have been impacted by the gospel over the centuries. Thousands upon thousands became a part of the church in the early stages of its history—all because 120 people were filled with the Holy Spirit and empowered as witnesses of the resurrection of Jesus Christ.

POWER FOR LIFE | IT'S MISSIONAL

We have to admit that it's possible to live out your life as a Christian and yet live an unproductive spiritual life. Some believers live for years and years and . . .

- Never personally lead anyone to faith in Christ.
- Never see anything supernatural happen in answer to their prayers.
- Never experience freedom from lingering habits and addictive patterns.
- Never sense the explosive release of the Holy Spirit's passion for the broken.
- Never feel the rush of the peace, joy, and strength that comes from His presence.

God's purpose for you involves so much more. He wants you to be part of a revolution to take over the world, not politically or economically but spiritually. He wants to rescue those trapped by sin and selfishness. He wants to protect people like Justin from certain death. He wants to heal and restore and reconnect people to a God who loves them. He wants to offer the world *proof* that He is alive through you.

Waiting for you is the adventure of following a living Jesus in what He is doing on planet earth today. This is the opportunity to be infused with, overwhelmed by, and baptized in the Holy Spirit. Waiting for you is the chance to see lives changed and miracles released into the world. Would you like to say that you . . .

- Personally led hundreds of people to faith in Christ?
- Prayed and saw the power of God released to heal someone who was sick?
- Experienced freedom from habits and addictions that held you in the past?
- Have known the explosive release of the Holy Spirit's joy and power in your life as you have worshipped Him?

Are you hungry for something more? Are you ready to be baptized in the Holy Spirit?

DISCUSSION QUESTIONS FOR CHAPTER NINE

1. What place on earth do you feel closest to God and the most in awe of His creation? What is the feeling you have when you are there?
2. Have you ever experienced a significant answer to prayer in your life that you would consider a miracle?
3. When God demonstrates His power in the world, what does that prove to people?
4. The Holy Spirit births in us passion for needs or people we previously may have cared little about. What burden has God birthed in your heart through the work of the Holy Spirit?
5. In what way could you let the Holy Spirit use you in this upcoming week?

CONCLUSION

O ne of my favorite memories as a little boy was our holiday visits to Grandma's house. The most poignant moment was walking through the front door and smelling all the pies and cookies she had been baking for us. As I write these words, I can almost smell the apple pie and chocolate chip cookies! It's making me hungry just thinking about it!

That's the same effect I hope this book has had upon you. My desire is to make you hungry for a greater work of the Holy Spirit in your life. I want you to hunger for the impact of a life that is lived full of the Spirit of God.

IF YOU HAVE YET TO EXPERIENCE THE BAPTISM IN THE HOLY SPIRIT.

I hope you'll ask Jesus to do what He promised to do in your life. Remember Jesus is the baptizer in the Holy Spirit. John the Baptist said, "*He* will baptize you with the Holy Spirit and fire" (Matthew 3:11, emphasis added).

So ask Jesus to do what He promised. He wants to fill you to overflowing with the Holy Spirit. He wants to saturate your life with the power and presence of God, like a sponge dipped in a bucket of water. Can you imagine it?

- Peace will flood every cell in your being.

- Joy will erupt from the depths of who you are.
- Like an electrical current flows through a wire to power an appliance, the Holy Spirit will flood through your being to empower your life.

You ask, is this really for me? Hear the word of the apostle Peter on the Day of Pentecost. "You will receive the gift of the Holy Spirit. The promise is for you and your children and for all who are far off— for all whom the Lord our God will call" (Acts 2:38–39).

Can it be any more clear? *This promise is for you!* Let me recommend some practical steps:

a. Set aside time for prayer and worship in a place where you can be alone and can sing and pray out loud.

b. Invite a friend or a spiritual leader (your pastor) or your small group to pray with you, especially someone who has been baptized with the Holy Spirit.

c. Ask Jesus to baptize you with the Holy Spirit. (You may want to have a pastor or leader pray over you at this point and have them ask Jesus to fill you with the Holy Spirit).

d. Verbalize your worship and prayers loud enough for you to hear yourself. Remember that the gateway to the release of God's power in your life is your lips.

e. Try to speak in tongues. Yes, you read that right. God will not speak in tongues for you. It is a step of faith that you must take. So try.

I got hung up on that last step. My thought was that if it was going to happen it would need to be much more dramatic than that. It would need to be an almost uncontrollable impulse. I would hardly be able to contain myself. It would not be me at all; it would be all God.

But remember that speaking in tongues is the first step in your new partnership with the Holy Spirit. God wants to do other supernatural things through you as well. Your willingness to step out in faith and act or speak is the way all the other miracles will happen in your life.

You need to tune into the Holy Spirit as you worship. When you sense or hear in your spirit any small syllables, just speak out what you hear. Remember that when a small child speaks their first words, they don't speak in full sentences. They speak just some simple words and phrases. Their speech isn't perfect. It doesn't have to be. It's a beginning and that's all that matters.

The same is true when you speak in tongues. It doesn't have to be perfect. No dad or mom says to a child, "No. That's not correct! It's not Da Da; it's Daddy. Say it again!" When the child says "Da Da," everyone goes crazy with joy because the child is beginning to talk. Your heavenly Father feels the same way about you.

You won't understand it. You won't be perfect at it. But that isn't really the point anyway. What's important is that the Holy Spirit is being released through you. He is praying through you. You are beginning to partner with Him to do something beyond the natural. As you step out in faith, Jesus fills you with the Holy Spirit.

Honestly, I can't wait for you to experience this! And when you do, I have provided a place to contact me at the end of this book. I would love to hear your story. Tell me what happens in your life as you ask Jesus to baptize you in the Holy Spirit.

MAYBE YOU HAVE BEEN BAPTIZED IN THE HOLY SPIRIT AT SOME POINT IN YOUR LIFE BUT YOU HAVEN'T STAYED ACTIVE IN YOUR PARTNERSHIP WITH THE HOLY SPIRIT.

Remember that the baptism in the Holy Spirit isn't designed to be an event you seek, experience, and then move on. It's designed to be a gateway into an entirely new way of life. It's about providing proof of the resurrection. It's about accessing the disposition, capacity, and companionship of the Holy Spirit. It's about being used of God to provide divine solutions for people in need.

You have to activate this process in your life:

1. Spend time daily in worship. Psalm 22 tells us that God inhabits or is enthroned upon the praises of His people. So invite Him to come and rest upon your life as you worship.

3. Pray in the Spirit and speak in tongues every day. This is what Paul said about his own life, "I thank God that I speak in tongues more than all of you" (1 Corinthians 14:18). He understood the impact this practice had on his spiritual life. Paul was transformed in his character, edified in his soul, empowered to do supernatural things, and strengthened in his effectiveness in prayer.

5. Begin to believe that God wants to use you in a mighty way. Don't just live to survive your life, live to make a difference. Live to be used of God.

FINALLY, IF YOU ARE ACTIVE IN ALL OF THIS,
I HOPE THIS BOOK HAS INSPIRED YOU TO BELIEVE
FOR EVEN MORE THAN EVER BEFORE.

You might want to become even more intentional in your walk with God. I would encourage you to schedule times where you step out to minister to others and believe God for His miraculous release.

- Plan to go on a mission trip
- Join a street ministry team
- Ask your pastor to join the prayer teams that lay hands on the sick at your church
- Visit hospitals and pray for someone in need
- Look for opportunities to be used at work, school, or in your neighborhood

God wants to do so much more in your life than what you have experienced. Since the Holy Spirit is God, He can do anything God can do. And since the Holy Spirit lives within you, He can do whatever God can do through your life. You become an active partner with Almighty God to see His power released on earth.

Again, I would love to hear from you as you take this journey forward with the Holy Spirit. May God use you to change the world, one life at a time by the power of His Spirit in your life.

ENDNOTES

1. Mark Batterson, *Wild Goose Chase: Reclaim the Adventure of Pursuing God* (Colorado Springs: Multnomah Books, 2008), 4

2. Francis Chan, *Forgotten God: Reversing Our Tragic Neglect of the Holy Spirit* (Colorado Springs: David C. Cook, 2009).

3. Jack Hayford Quotes - http://www.azquotes.com/quote/1395306

4. George Stormont, *Smith Wigglesworth, a Man Who Walked with God* (Tulsa, OK: Harrison House, 2010), 39.

5. Petmeds.org

6. Andrew Murray, *Absolute Surrender* (West Conshohocken, PA: Infinity, 2014), 35.

7. Bruce Wilkinson, *You Were Born for This: Seven Keys for Predictable Miracles* (Colorado Springs: Multnomah, 2011), 45.

8. Chris Hodges, *Fresh Air: Trading Stale Spiritual Obligation for a Life-Altering, Energizing, Experience-It-Everyday Relationship with God* (Carol Stream, IL: Tyndale Momentum, 2012).

9. Rick Warren, *Purpose Driven Life: What on Earth Am I Here For?* (Grand Rapids, MI: Zondervan, 2002).

10. Martin Luther King Jr., https://www.brainyquote.com/quotes/quotes/m/martinluth105087.html?src=t_step

ABOUT THE AUTHOR

Jeff Leake has served as the lead pastor of Allison Park Church for twenty-five years. He is also the leader of Reach Northeast, a church planting movement that has planted more than 120 churches. Jeff holds an MA in missiology from the Assemblies of God Theological Seminary. He is the author of four books: *God in Motion, The Question That Changed My Life, Learning to Follow Jesus,* and *Praying with Confidence.* He and his wife, Melodie, reside in Allison Park, PA. They have been married for over twenty-eight years and have five children and one grandchild.

FOR MORE INFORMATION

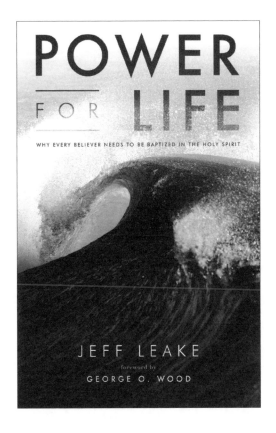

For more information about this and other valuable resources visit
WWW.MYHEALTHYCHURCH.COM

To share your story with the author visit
MYSTORY@JEFFLEAKEPOWERFORLIFE.COM

ADDITIONAL RESOURCES FOR	Additional messages on this topic
CHURCH LEADERS ARE AVAILABLE AT	Video trailer series
WWW.JEFFLEAKEPOWERFORLIFE.COM	Coaching for church leaders
THESE INCLUDE:	Video testimonies